From Sea to Shining Sea

William G. Tanner, Compiler

BROADMAN PRESS

Nashville, Tennessee

Unless otherwise indicated, all Scripture references are from the King James Version of the Holy Bible.

Scripture references marked (GNB) are from the *Good News Bible,* the Bible in Today's English Version. Old Testament: Copyright © American Bible Society 1976; New Testament: Copyright © American Bible Society 1966, 1971, 1976. Used by permission.

Scripture references marked (NASB) are from the *New American Standard Bible.* Copyright © The Lockman Foundation, 1960, 1962, 1963, 1968, 1971, 1972, 1973, 1977. Used by permission.

Scripture references marked (RSV) are from the Revised Standard Version of the Bible, copyrighted 1946, 1952 ©1971, 1973.

Dewey Decimal Classification: 266.022
Subject Headings: MISSIONS, HOME // HOME MISSION BOARD
Library of Congress Catalog Card Number: 86-9609
Printed in the United States of America

Library of Congress Cataloging-in-Publication Data

From Sea to shining sea.

    1. Missions, Home. 2. Southern Baptist Convention—Missions—United States. 3. Baptists—Missions—United States. I. Tanner, William Graydon, 1930-
BV2520.F76 1986   266'.6132   86-9609
ISBN 0-8054-5667-8

Dedication

to our Home Missionaries . . .
those thousands of people who, from
1845 to 1986, have given without
question their energies, their
talents, and in many instances
their whole lives for the
cause of reaching
America for Christ

Pastors and other mission communicators have long expressed a need for home mission sermons and illustrations. This book, *From Sea to Shining Sea*, will help to meet that need.

All of the chapters relate to the purpose, objectives, and tasks of the Home Mission Board, Southern Baptist Convention. They are presented in such a way to help the reader understand the work of the largest domestic missionary agency in the world . . . as well as to equip the reader to pass on this thrilling story to other audiences.

Contents

1
What the Bible Says About Ministry
Luke 4:18-19

Paul R. Adkins

Christian social ministries, a major program of the Home Mission Board, serves as a connection between the caring faith of loving Christians and a world desperately needing love and care. These ministries may be expressed in Baptist centers, church community weekday ministries, literacy ministries, youth and family services, migrant and seasonal farm workers, disaster relief and domestic hunger, alcohol and drug abusers, and prison ministries. Underlying all these actions is a working philosophy based squarely on the Bible's teachings, including:

God's Revelatory Process

Jesus came as the crown of the Father's revelation. He reminds us that all persons are created in the mirror-image of God as the crowning act of God's creative work. People are able to have a relationship with their God.

The Bible puts it this way: "And Christ became a human being and lived here on earth among us and was full of loving forgiveness and truth" (John 1:14, TLB).

This human relationship is based on God Who sent a human being to identify with mankind forever. There is no individual life or arena of life that God's concern does not penetrate and permeate. He seeks to bring light to all darkness.

The Worth of Persons

The value of persons is given new meaning by the life and teaching of Jesus. He teaches that one human life is worth more than the world itself. Jesus looks upon everyone as being of supreme value. He never met an unimportant person. One indication of this was Jesus' treatment of the outcasts of His day, especially women and children. He said, "Let the little children come to me, and don't prevent them. For of such is the Kingdom of Heaven" (Matt. 19:14, TLB).

The Principle of Love Put to Action

Jesus clearly stated that godly love includes everyone, even one's enemies. Our love is to be shown in kind and degree to the love which God expresses for us. Jesus said, "And so I am giving a new commandment to you now—love each other just as much as I love you. Your strong love for each other will prove to the world that you are my disciples" (John 13:34-35, TLB).

The love of Jesus enables His disciples to love not only the neighbor-neighbor, but the enemy-neighbor and the stranger-neighbor.

The Nature of the Christian Experience

It is within any person's power to accept or reject God as the center of one's love and devotion. One can opt for wholeness as a complete person by responding to God. This wholeness is the basis of redeemed persons' being able to minister to those who lack the path to wholeness.

The lost person becomes a new creature or creation in

Christ as a result of repentance, faith, and forgiveness. The new creature is then able to assert that the forgiveness of God may be viewed as the most powerful healing agent in the world.

This healing can be communicated through a life-style and value system that portrays this wholeness. Jesus, the Master Teacher, declared, "My purpose is to give life in all its fullness" (John 10:10, TLB).

The Gospel Through Persons

People respond to Christians who have motives to serve them in the name of Christ *if* first we are significant to them. Only as we dare to expose ourselves to others will our work, witness, and worship begin to mean something for Christ.

God knew this when He entrusted the good news of Christ to the disciples. Modern disciples continue the tradition of being the channels of hope to a hopeless world. The modern disciple is like Paul in that, as God says, "He is a chosen instrument to take my message to the nations" (Acts 9:15, TLB).

The Example of Jesus

Jesus began His ministry by announcing, "The Spirit of the Lord is upon me; . . . he has sent me to heal the broken-hearted and to announce that captives shall be released and the blind shall see, that the downtrodden shall be freed from their oppressors and that God is ready to give blessings to all who come to him" (Luke 4:18-19, TLB).

Jesus had a compelling force to minister to people with special need for what He could do for them. In Christian social ministries, those who minister give themselves in caring by meeting needs which may be physical, in order to reach the point at which their spiritual help will also be accepted.

The Equality of Those in Need

Ministers of social concern in the name of Christ know the Bible does not allow for the common distinctions made by some. There can be no consideration of which clients are more "deserving" or likely to respond. In extending the Lord's ministry in its outward working, people's needs, and not their station in life, should dictate our efforts toward reaching them spiritually and physically.

Those in need have an equality before those who minister to them. They know what James taught, "If ye fulfill the royal law according to the scripture, Thou shalt love thy neighbour as thyself, you do well. But if ye have respect to persons, ye commit sin, and are convicted of the law as transgressors" (Jas. 2:8-9, KJV).

The Church's Responsibility

Many persons believe that the church does not care for them because Christians have seemed too heartless in meeting their needs. They ask: "Is the church afraid to get involved? Should the church be set on a hill away from the needs of men?"

The Bible gives clear instruction to church members which can aid in answering those charges with positive action. Even in the selection of deacons, the early Christians gave precedence to physical needs. This is evident in Acts 6:1-2, "With the believers multiplying rapidly, there were rumblings of discontent. Those who spoke only Greek complained that their widows were being discriminated against, that they were not being given as much food, in the daily distribution, as the widows who spoke Hebrew. So the Twelve called a meeting of all the believers" (TLB).

Love In Action

Love "in deed and in truth" is more than a motto. To withhold from the needy food and clothing is bad enough, but it is far worse to withhold from them the good which the gospel can give. Christian social ministries propose to see that even the poor have the gospel preached to them. This is evidenced in 1 John 3:17-18, "But if someone who is supposed to be a Christian has money enough to live well, and sees a brother in need, and won't help him—how can God's love be within him? Little children, let us stop just saying we love people; let us really love them, and show it by our actions" (TLB).

Partial Basis for Judgment

From the mouth of Jesus, it is clear the responsible discipleship is more than verbal assent to a set of affirmations. Jesus said, "Not all who sound religious are really godly people. They may refer to me as 'Lord' but still won't get to heaven. For the decisive question is whether they obey my Father in heaven" (Matt. 7:21, TLB). In Matthew 25's scene of judgment, Jesus makes it clear that separation of the "sheep" and "goats" (v. 31) will be based on helping or refusing to help other human beings.

Christian social ministries is based squarely on biblical teachings. They are thoroughly New Testament. A principle is only a principle, however. The New Testament reminds the disciple constantly that Christ is still present, in "the

least of these my brothers" (Matt. 25:45, TLB). Will you be
a part of that presence?

Paul R. Adkins, Associate Director
Mission Ministries
Home Mission Board

2
The World in Our Midst
Acts 1:8
Robert T. Banks

And ye shall be witnesses unto me (Acts 1:8).

Thomas Wolfe wrote, "You can't go home again." After thirty years my wife and I went back to Georgia to serve with the Home Mission Board. But, it's true, you really can't go home again. Things have changed—they just are not the same anymore. As we returned to Georgia, I tried to reminisce and remember some of the things I had known in my boyhood. The railroad trestle, from which we jumped into the Towalaga River, is not as "high" as it used to be. The old creek down by the country church I grew up in is not as "wide" as it once was. In fact, the First Baptist Church auditorium is not as "overwhelming" in size as I remember it. And, the kerosene lanterns, the water well with its bucket, and the path out back of the church ain't no more. Well, there are some things you don't want to come home to.

I have found that my home state and the South are changing. The South is and has been the stronghold of Southern Baptists. However, I think we need to take note that from 1970 to 1980 the United Methodists and the Catholics outgrew Southern Baptists in the South. Southern Baptist churches grew by 1.3 percent, the United Methodists by 3.5 percent, and the Catholics by 7 percent. Baptists grew in membership by 10.9 percent, Methodists by 10.4 percent, and Catholics by 15.6 percent. I remember growing up in

Georgia knowing only one Catholic boy in our small town, Charlie. But now in the community where I live most are Catholic. My world is different.

I remember when I was a boy we would go to the grocery store or the filling station to listen to the Yankees talk when they stopped while driving through. The way they talked was strange. But now most of the people in my subdivision are people from "up North." Things change.

There were 20,000 ethnics in Georgia in 1970. In 1980, there were more than one hundred thousand ethnics, and more than sixty thousand of these were Hispanics. There are now sounds that I did not hear in my youth. There are life-styles of which I had no knowledge. Things are different.

You can't go home again doesn't mean that home is worse. It may be better, but you have to recognize that it is different —it's changed. Another thing you have to recognize is that "home" is a mission field. About 53 percent of the Georgia population is unchurched, and that may be representative of the old South. Home is a mission field! The world is in our midst.

I would like to mention five things concerning the Home Mission Board's relationship and responsibility to the world in our midst.

The first thing I want to note is that ethnics are responding to the gospel. Listen to these facts:

1. A new Korean Southern Baptist church is begun every three weeks; there are now 321 in the United States.
2. In 1983 more than 27,000 professions of faith were recorded by language-culture congregations; that's three professions of faith per hour.
3. The Southern Baptist Convention has the largest

Spanish-speaking evangelistic religious group in the world.

4. Since 1975, Southern Baptists in the United States have resettled more than 10,000 refugees from various countries, resulting in 281 language-culture congregations.

God is blessing and ethnics are responding throughout this land. I am amazed at what I read and what I hear about how ethnics are being won to Christ and how congregations are being started.

I believe we must seek to move quickly and definitively into the areas where God is working. Our experience in missions has been that we do not always have the luxury of long-term opportunities. Today's mission field may be tomorrow's closed door. We face the imperative of immediacy.

Second, *we cannot determine or control where God does His work.* Sometimes we think we would like to, but we can't. As Christians, we must be open to God's leadership. We cannot control all that takes place nor should we want to. We can't do it from state offices, and we can't do it from Atlanta.

It seems to me that we must be strategists and facilitators, that is, people who make things possible. We need to be catalysts, and even perhaps need to be change agents, out on the cutting edge where God is working. Our mission money, money that Southern Baptists give, must help to assist and facilitate the equipping of leadership, the beginning of new congregations, and their move toward self-support and missions. Our money must help to make all of this possible.

Third, *ethnic leaders must see themselves reaching out on mission.* Those to whom missionaries are sent must become missionaries, too, not simply in their own communities where their primary concern might be, but throughout this land. Jimmy Anderson, an Indian missionary in Oklahoma, took a group of twelve from six Indian churches from around Shawnee, Oklahoma, to an Indian reservation in California. They traveled 1,500 miles, stayed seven days, slept on the concrete floor of the tribal community building, cooked their own food, but also led Bible studies and helped in revival services. About thirty-five attended the daily Vacation Bible School, sixty attended the evening worship, and nineteen persons came to accept Christ as Savior. And there is a whole lot more. Those to whom missionaries are sent must become missionaries, too, not just where they live, but they must have a love that comes to embrace this whole land and the entire world.

Fourth, *Bold Mission Thrust in our land cannot be viable or realized without a priority on ethnic work.* The cities cannot be reached without addressing the needs of language persons. The cities must be addressed not at a particular point but in a comprehensive way. Many of you have heard of "Mega Focus Cities Project" involving several Southern Baptist Convention agencies and the fifty largest cities in this country. It is designed to bring together all of the interests of the cities and to do such in a comprehensive and cohesive way in order to reach the cities, which is a priority.

Fifth, *the HMB's great problem, as is yours, is trying to respond to all opportunities that come to us.* Ethnic work is not a simple thing. We have heard that time and time again. It is complex, made so by language, culture, numbers, lack of trained leaders, non-Baptist background, and so forth. But we must respond to those opportunities God has placed before us.

Part of what we are dealing with, it seems to me, is what I would like to call "Wellness in Missions." You have heard of wellness related to health. It's a concept finding its application among the medical professionals, social-service people, educators, and others concerned about the health and well-being of individuals and society. The concept deals with the realization that behavior or life-style, not medical services, is the primary determinant of health. Wellness is not static; it is dynamic, moving toward fulfillment and potential. If I were to transfer that concept and relate it to the church, I would say the wellness of a church may be determined by its behavior, its life-style; that is, what it does out of the foundations of its beliefs rather than out of what it says it believes.

Wellness is a mission life-style. It is behavior and life-style on the part of the congregation. Wellness in missions as applied to ethnic work is the promoting and supporting of well-being and movement toward greater fulfillment in God's plan. It is not saying that all churches should be in conformity. That's not Scriptural or Baptistic. It's not saying that ethnic churches ought to be like Anglo churches. I'd have to say that is not wellness. I would define wellness in missions like this: It is an active process through which the congregation becomes aware of and makes choices toward a more successful existence and mission. These choices are greatly influenced by biblical teachings, leadership, and the congregation's own self-concept within parameters of culture and environment. Each develops a unique mission life-style which changes or is changed by the reflections of its leaders, the congregation's spiritual depth, the physical properties (not merely property but properties), and its social/cultural heritage. Wellness, growth, dynamic, fulfillment, culture, life-style, mission!

I would like to say that the Home Mission Board must, and I believe will, put dollars where the priorities are. We cannot afford the luxury of trying to do everything at the same priority level. Evangelism, ministry, and new work are where the priorities are. And this includes language work. The question that sometimes comes is, "Must the Home Mission Board put dollars where results are, not neglecting our total mission work and needs, but being responsive to where God is working?" I agree with Dr. Gerald Palmer, vice-president of the Home Mission Board, that in some way we must reach the point where we can provide flexible funding so that as plans and needs develop, we may be able to respond much faster than through a long planning period. We need to respond to what God does in His timetable and not ours.

We must use funds judiciously and appropriately. Our funds are limited and are entrusted to us by the Southern Baptist Convention by people who give sacrificially. Plans must be made and implemented to reach people. We must pray and find God's directions, but we must do our homework. We must seek to find where the needs are, then plan and seek to implement those plans to reach people. The Home Mission Board and Southern Baptists have allocated funds to help reach people, but if we don't adequately do our planning, and don't seek to implement those plans, those funds, frankly, may be lost. We are in the business of trying to reach people and must seek to utilize those resources that Southern Baptists provide for us within a time frame so we may be able to reach out and help people to know Christ as Savior.

Inter-agency cooperation is a necessity. The Home Mission Board has the responsibility for the maintenance and viability of the programs assigned to it by the Southern Baptist Convention. We can never do it alone. The Home Mission Board, other SBC agencies, and the state conventions are interdependent, in fact, locked together. We cannot be isolated from each other, if we ever could. Yes, the Home Mission Board gets credit for many things, but when the story is really known, other agencies, particularly the state conventions, have helped to make it possible. It's not merely our achievement; it's their achievement. As we begin to work together more, we must come to the place where, as things happen on the Convention level, that the states become involved in the process more and more. We need to communicate with each other about what is being done and what is coming about. There are some new directions in missions, and we must cooperate to get the job done. We work with philosophy, programming, plans, materials, and many other things, and must work together, perhaps as never before, to do the job God has for us. Agencies must also work together in evangelism, ministry, and church starting. Normal responses will not meet the needs. We must find ways to reach people.

Furthermore, the Home Mission Board is moving into new frontiers. In updating its long-range plans, Target AD 2000, the Home Mission Board will consider a new objective or ministry. It is this, "To challenge and equip all Southern Baptists to minister to meet the needs of persons." Ministry is actually not the purview of any one program. It doesn't belong to Language and it doesn't belong to Christian Social Ministries. It doesn't belong to any one program at the Home Mission Board. Ministry, evangelizing, and congrega- tionalizing are shared by all programs, and they are comple- mentary to one another. Ministry is vital to all of our work. It serves to meet the needs of persons but also helps in winning people to Christ and in beginning churches.

We must come to view the wholeness we are about. From the outside, many times the Home Mission Board is seen by its parts, not as a total thrust. Sometimes a program seems larger than the agency. One task is to help people see that what we are about is a total thrust in trying to reach the country for Christ. Turf building at one end of the field may mean that erosion may occur at the other, but ultimately the turf topsoil is also undermined. We must learn to work together on a state level, Convention-wide level, between agencies, and within the Home Mission Board. Wherever we are, we must move together if we are going to do what God wants us to do.

A part is not larger than the whole, of course. A leader is not larger than the part. I'm not bigger than good administration at the board; I'm not bigger than the inter-agency relationships which are ours. The part is not larger than the whole, and the leader is not larger than the part. If we are to win this land for Christ, we must do it together. Dr. William G. Tanner, president of the Home Mission Board, has said that we need to develop a cohesive and comprehensive missions and evangelism strategy, and that is where we are moving.

The Home Mission Board has considered a new strategy. It reads, "The agency will lead in enlistment and development of leadership from among the people served, recognizing them as full participants in Southern Baptist life." The implications are many. This is a big assignment to lay on ourselves, and it will not be easy to make changes. It will not happen as quickly as some would want, but it must be done. Candidly, some of the biggest problems revolve around ourselves, our own attitudes, our unwillingness to facilitate the work, and many other factors. I suspect that ethnic fellowships have developed for many good reasons, but I also suspect that perhaps some have come about because they are products of our own attitudes and unwillingness to give expression to what God is doing among these fellowships.

A part of the strategy I read to you stated, "Recognizing them as full participants in Southern Baptist life." We cannot preach full participation, or even partnership, and at the same time practice paternalism. It is not where ethnic people are or want to be. It does not serve us well, and it certainly does not serve God well.

I pray that God will give us a vision and hearts and feet

to match that vision. I pray that He might give us new eyes
to see—to see the world in our midst.

Robert T. Banks, Executive Vice-president
Home Mission Board

3

Am I My Brother's Keeper?
The Bible and Ministering
Genesis 4:6-9

M. Wendell Belew

Christian ministry has its beginning in Genesis and with the relationship of Cain and Abel. "And the Lord said to Cain, Why are you angry? And why is your countenance fallen? If you do well, will not your countenance be lifted up and if you do not well, sin is crouching at the door; and its desire is for you, but you must master it.' And Cain told Abel, his brother, and it came about when they were in the field that Cain rose up against Abel his brother and killed him. Then the Lord said to Cain, 'Where is Abel, your brother?' And he said, 'I do not know. Am I my brother's keeper?' And He said, 'What have you done? The voice of your brother's blood is crying to Me from the ground" (Gen. 4:6-9, NASB).

The concept of Christian ministry, as promoted by the HMB, begins with time and life itself. It is represented in the controversy of mankind's relationships—of anger, murder, and responsibility of brother to brother.

What is this responsibility? "Am I my brother's keeper?"

It took the Hebrew nation a long time to realize that they were their brother's keeper. Ministry is not a dominant theme in the Old Testament. Most often, when something unpleasant happened to a person, it was considered a result of the individual's having sinned. The "friends" of Job came to encourage him to confess all the wrong he had done. Even in that time it was easier to condemn than to care.

The Ten Commandments show God's effort to delineate morality (Ex. 20:1-17). Societies have always needed some basis of law from which they could determine their values and responsibilities. These Commandments were expanded, and they established personal and property rights and relational responsibilities to God, family, and neighbors. The Hebrews assumed the inferiority of women and accepted the position of slavery. This tradition was pretty well perpetuated throughout the Old Testament and is somewhat to the present day.

Yet from the Old Testament and the Book of Leviticus come the words, "love your neighbor as yourself" (Lev. 19:18, NASB). Not just brother, or just brother's keeper, but *neighbor*. Love was then introduced as the sum of this moral and ethical code of behavior. It was given to a primitive people who were finding their way as a nation and a people of God.

"Love your neighbor as yourself" (NASB) emerges as the sum value of the law and was repeated in Matthew 22:39 as Jesus announced the Great Commandment.

Jesus proclaimed the fulfillment of the law by saying, "You shall love the Lord your God with all your heart, and with all your soul and with all your mind. This is the great and foremost commandment. The second is like it, you shall love your neighbor as yourself. On these two commandments depend the whole Law and the Prophets" (vv. 37-40, NASB).

This then is a marvelous commentary on what is intended for mankind. Jesus exemplifies His prophetic stance by summing it all up in the context of love. If you love God with all you are, and you love your neighbor as yourself, the commandments fall into perspective and give us the recognition that God truly is love. He does not hate or condemn us, for He sent His only begotten Son that whoever would believe in Him would not perish (see John 3:16). He does not judge harshly. He recognizes that we will not be perfect, and He promises us that we have an Advocate, "Christ Jesus the righteous."

What did the early church do about loving and about the legal imprints of God upon mankind? The church had to make some cultural changes. Love enemies? Pray for them? The church had to make way for diverse methods of reaching the lost. There may have been discussions over which method of evangelism was more correct. Was it the method at Pentecost? Or was it more correct as practiced by Peter and John with the lame man at the Beautiful Gate? Was there a growing dichotomy between "evangelism" and "ministry"?

Jesus would not seek to separate "ministry" from "evangelism." There is a difficulty in discussing or using the word *ministry*. We have employed it so often to symbolize pastorates, ordained types and not so much "servanthood." Jesus was a Servant, and He ministered. Some of His most devoted followers were women. He would announce that all the bonds were broken, that there were no slaves, no masters, no male, no female, no Gentile, no Jew. That position of Jesus would be a hard one to accept by all of the Judaizers and even by Christians through 2,000 years.

Jesus stopped to minister to all kinds of people. On some occasions they would find eternal life. On others they would hear the answers but would turn away. As the rich young ruler came to Him and asked, "What must I do to inherit eternal life?" Jesus told him to sell what he had and give it to the poor. This was not the same answer that Jesus gave to Nicodemus, "You must be born again" (John 3:7, NASB). And yet perhaps it was a similar answer. Jesus would minister to the woman with an issue of blood. He ministered to Zaccheus who had climbed into a sycamore tree (though He went home with him for dinner first). He ministered to the lame and the blind, and He would ultimately call them "witnesses" and send them forth to minister as He had been sent. Later called them a "royal priesthood" (1 Pet. 2:9). In reading Exodus and Leviticus one discovers that priests had to be whole. They could not have a crippled hand or foot or be lame. Jesus makes high priests and ministers out of everybody! We are all given talents and gifts with which to minister.

Sometimes Jesus spoke of loving and of caring when it had nothing to do with salvation, except as the act would evidence the love of Christ. That's the case with the story of the Good Samaritan. To my knowledge nobody was saved there, but many of us have been encouraged by the story and have learned that religious titles do not make us minister or teach us to be our "brother's keeper."

Paul emphasized the supremacy of the gift of love and responsibility to rulers, the church, and the world.

The early church would grapple with what is missions and what is evangelism? In the mighty event at Pentecost, 3,000 people were saved and heard the good news in their own language. A few hours later the number would grow to 5,000, because a lame man who was sitting at the Beautiful Gate was healed.

Jesus said, "[I have] come to seek and to save that which was lost" (Luke 19:10). He said, "[I have] come not to be ministered unto, but to minister" (Matt. 20:28), and, "As my Father hath sent me, even so send I you" (John 20:21).

The early church began to practice something of caring. The incident of caring for the Greek widows brought about the appointment of the Seven. Later the church became concerned about orphans, the sick, and the aged.

Widows were in a terrible plight in that day. If a widow's husband died, she lost all her estate, and unless a son or other relative took her in, she had nothing. Lepers had to go about the streets crying, "unclean, unclean," so no one would touch them. If someone loved them they might leave food at the edge of the city dump where the lepers could find it. Those beset by terminal illnesses were often simply cast aside.

The story is told of the early church at Carthage when the city was beset with a plague and many people were dying. Everyone was frightened. But the little band of Christians went out into the streets and gathered up the bodies and buried them. They ministered to those who were sick. The city was so impressed that the church became successful, so successful that it built a church house and forgot what its real purpose was. The church in its struggle to become successful sometimes forgets to be its "brother's keeper."

About 300 years after Christ, Christianity became eminently successful as Constantine accepted Christ. Christianity became respectable and soon the state captured evangelism. That is, the state church announced that its citizens were Christians. As a Christian nation, everyone who was a citizen of the nation was considered to be Christian. Evangelism became a state function, and the head of state became the head of Christianity. Over a millennium would sweep by before the church recovered from its evangelistic captivity by the state. Little Christian orders were formed by those who were caring and who wanted to see that there were rights and justice. They ministered to the underprivileged. They established orders that ministered to orphans and provided food and clothing for the poor.

They built hospitals, and the church again became, in gifted parts, a ministering body. Yet the church officially remained in captivity by the state.

Oddly enough, the change in the church took place as laypersons became aware of what was going on in the world.

Captain James Cook was making explorations of the world. William Carey, a cobbler, became concerned about the plight of people who lived outside the influence of state churches and asked that his Baptist association might send him. He originally wanted to go to the Sandwich Islands, but the Lord led him to India. He began his ministry by caring for people. He translated the Bible into many different dialects and languages. His ministry was evangelism; his evangelism was ministry. Americans inspired by what was taking place and moved by the Spirit of God, sent Adoniram Judson and his wife, Ann Hasseltine, to join Carey, but they were led to Burma instead. When the Judsons were isolated for awhile on the Ile de France, Ann saw one of her neighbors beating a slave and she intervened. The next morning the slave owner had the young woman slave in terrible shackles and irons. Ann intervened again and sought to have the slave set free. In Burma she ministered to the people who were burdened, lost, and ill of many diseases. Some were saved.

Thus began the great modern mission effort of taking the good news to the world. Missionaries would be sent to the corners of the earth, and they too could minister and evangelize as they chose. Along the frontier in America were revivalistic expressions which caused Baptists, Methodists, and Presbyterians to grow tremendously from East to West. As churches were established they would sometimes care for the orphans and the widows and occasionally would be concerned about blacks, Hispanics, Indians, and migrants. Sometimes the church leaders considered ministering as not really being a part of what they were as a church. The "church" was easier to count from the standpoint of how many people made decisions in a revival or attended a Vacation Bible School, or how large the budget was.

Now history is reversed in that ministry in large measure

captured by the state. By and large, the state feeds the poor
and builds hospitals. The state takes care of orphans and
looks after migrants. Nations of the Western world have
assumed ministry. The church has retaken evangelism and
preaches that perspective as though it were the only recourse
for the church. Sometimes Christians fail to remember the
ministry of the Incarnate Christ. Too often we forget Jesus,
the Living Word, and many great acts of God are missed. His
redemptive plan in the written Word, in the history of mankind, and in the lives of those to whom and with whom we
minister is often not seen. Much of the Word of God we
know has come from loving and being loved by others. This
exchange and interchange make the body of Christ real and
cause us to expand the parameters and to dare us to risk in
His name. Because of God's love we may venture to do that
which has not been done before and to do it in His name,
remembering it is not important that our names be known
but that His name be glorified.

It is much easier to preach at the world than it is to serve
the world and to become a part of the suffering, the lostness,
the loneliness, and the dislocation of people. For the church
to grow, nothing must override the fact that Christ has come
to all people, and He will come again. Those of us who know
Him will rejoice at that and will not need to manipulate the
time of His coming or the place, for He said that no one
knows that.

To some Christians there is a conflict between "evangelism" and "ministry" or between witnessing as a preach-
ment or an action of being our "brother's keeper."

To some Christians, being their "brother's keeper" is
enough without the overriding love of Jesus being proclaimed.

Shall we preach to them that Christ came to save that
which was lost or to minister rather than to be ministered

to? He sent us to deal with these two facets of the Great Commandment; to love God with all we are, and to love our fellowman as we love ourselves.

Three billion people in our world are not Christians. About that same number do not have enough to eat. One hundred million people in the United States do not claim to be Christians. Twenty million of these are poor. Two million are homeless. Over twenty-five million are over the age of sixty-five. Do we preach to them? Or minister to them?

God expects us to know that we are our brother's keeper —but our brother can only be kept in the name of God's Son, Jesus. This is the fulfillment of the Great Commandment. And He said, "As my Father has sent me, even so send I you"—to seek to save that which was lost—and to minister "as my brother's keeper."

M. Wendell Belew, Director
Missions Ministries Division
Home Mission Board

4
Now Is the Time
Ecclesiastes 3:1-8

Robert E. Bingham

Forty years ago I found myself at the United States Naval Academy. I had expected to study damage control, navigation, seamanship, engineering, and the like. But one class was learning how to type. What a letdown this seemed at the time. However, the content matter for learning how to type in those days has been an aid to my personal growth. For you see, what I was typing was the age-old slogan, "Now is the time for all good men to come to the aid of their party."

To center our attention on home missions today, I would like the liberty of paraphrasing that slogan to read, "Now is the time for all good persons to come to the aid of their country."

I claim no pride of authorship in that statement. Hundreds of years ago "The Preacher" in the Book of Ecclesiastes, chapter 3, verses 1-8, claimed there was a time for everything and a special time for specific matters.

Now Is the Time . . . Why?

Amos is one of my favorite Old Testament characters. He may have been the first recorded "moonlighter," for certainly he had two jobs and perhaps three. He was not one of the affluent personages of his day, but certainly one of the most courageous. While Amos was tending the sheep the Lord spoke to him and told him he was to go to Bethel, the capital of the Northern Kingdom. He was to prophesy there that the Lord God would hold the people of Israel accountable for their sins.

Amos must have had that "Who-me?" expression on his face. He tried to make some excuse to avoid the calling of God. He was an unlettered man, uncultured in the tastes of the sophisticated Hebrews of his day, a Southerner who felt quite uncomfortable going across the "Mason-Dixon Line" of his day into the Northern Kingdom to expose the sins of his unfriendly brethren.

Yet, in due time, he found himself in the marketplace of the city, trying to prophesy to the elders and the aristocrats of that community. He laid upon them the charges of corruption in high places, immorality of both husbands and wives, greed, and dishonesty in the marketplace. His listeners took interest which turned to glee when he said that God would bring judgment upon the Philistines, upon Tyre, Sidon, Edom, and his own country, Judah. It was only then that he finally apprised the Israelites that God was not going to put up with their sins any more than He was going to indulge their neighboring countries.

When we read this account our minds shift to sinful Russia, godless China, the greedy Mideastern countries, and perhaps to bigoted Ireland. But when we do so, we're not only setting up straw men, we are playing children's games.

Let me speak to you in adult language today. My wife and I were pleased to visit a friend we met at the Baptist World Congress and were privileged to have him in our home for a week. When we returned his invitation to visit him in Ireland, we did not realize how close his home was to the no-man's-land in Belfast. Machine-gun fire and bombings were heard within our earshot each night. There were reported killings in the morning newspaper. And finally, I confessed to him at breakfast on our last day, "Dane, Opha and I want you to know that we will continue praying for you and Beth as you live in such trauma and turmoil."

He responded in typical British politeness, "Bob, it is interesting that you should say that. You see, Beth and I have been praying for you and Opha for several years as we have read in the newspapers that Atlanta has more people killed by homicide each year than have been killed in any one year of the Irish rebellion!"

As you see, the need for missions and for God's Spirit to be alive in the world came home to roost in my beloved city. Now, in case you are resting comfortably in the sinfulness of Atlanta, let me read for you some headlines and first paragraphs of articles in your own daily newspaper. (At this time, I open the current day's newspaper and actually read accounts of gross sin and immorality in their own community.) And, now, you see, it has even come closer home than Atlanta. It has come home to Your Town, U.S.A.

If you still wonder why "now is the time," hear these unsettling statistics:

• Saudi Arabia is continuing to pour millions of dollars for the evangelization of the United States to a Muslim understanding of God. In 1980, it was 50 million dollars. Since then there have not been reported figures, but there has been increasing Muslim activity in our nation.

• Arnold Toynbee in his classic treatise on the history of civilizations wrote, "No republic has endured longer than 200 years whose roots were not firmly entrenched in Almighty God." Even a poor mathematician can figure out that America's time is at hand. An astute observer of the moral and spiritual conditions of our nation can make even more critical prophecies about the future of our nation.

• The Mormons have come out of the backwoods and the states of Utah-Wyoming-Arizona-Colorado to the main streets of Atlanta and Dallas. Indeed, massive, new Mormon temples have come into prominence in these two of the Bible Belt's most prestigious cities.

Now Is the Time . . . Where?

The Home Mission Board's strategy for placing mission personnel throughout the nation, when reduced to its least common denominator, might be: Place the missionaries *where the people are* and *where the churches are not.* At first glance, it might seem that we could easily determine where our missionaries should be sent when there are approximately 3,700 of them to be supported with a 70-million-dollar budget. But let me ask you, "If all 3,700 missionaries and all of the 70 million dollars of financial resources were targeted in on your state alone, do you think we could guarantee the evangelization of your state?" I have not found a congregation which felt that could be reliably predicted. Therefore, the leadership at the Home Mission Board, under Dr. Tanner's guidance, must find a strategy to use our scarce resources amid a sinful and needy nation.

We must be good stewards of what financial and human resources are available to our agency. We thank God for churches like yours who provide almost all of the human and financial resources we have. By your generosity we are able to have funds with which to do our work of trying to bring our beloved land to the feet of Jesus for His saving grace and redemption. No longer can we have a missionary couple on an Indian reservation with a total population of about three thousand Indians, of whom only thirty might be in attendance at the Baptist church on Sunday morning. Rather, we have found that we need to use missionary couples to be catalytic missionaries with the lay leadership already on the reservations to involve the indigenous principle of leading the community with a person of common cultural background. We have found by supplying the catalytic missionary with an airplane that he can visit six to eight reservations with regularity. He can give encouragement and training to the pastor who provides leadership to the local congregation. In effect, what this has done is to free five or six missionary couples to work in other areas of our nation where there are more people and fewer churches.

(Note: You may wish to give some specific examples of where mission work is being done through your Home Mission Board. Many examples are throughout this book. Choose these on the basis of the congregation's needs and the heart of the sermon you are preaching. May God bless your efforts.)

Now Is the Time . . . How?

Some of you are already thinking ahead of me and saying to yourself, *Here comes the money pitch!* I wouldn't want to disappoint you in any way, and to relieve your mind, you can be assured that we cannot exist without your financial support. But there's far more to it than that.

I see the support of the Home Mission Board as three "P's" in a pod. The first "P" is our *Program.* Actually, we have thirteen programs of work authorized by the Southern Baptist Convention whereby we are directed to do mission and evangelistic work in our nation. These vary from mass evangelistic strategy to Christian social ministries, from various types of chaplaincy ministries to granting church loans for starting new buildings. I believe you will find the Home Mission Board's program statement to be strong and effective.

The second "P" would stand for *People.* Dr. Tanner has

stated many times that we must place our great emphasis upon enabling people to do the work for which God has called them. There are more people volunteering for vocational Home Mission work today than we have resources for placing them. You would be rightfully proud of the quality and the spiritual strength of these people who feel God wants them to be a part of the redemption of America.

The third "P" stands for *Pocketbook*. Our country has not yet come to grips with the lostness of our population. If so, we would not be spending three times as much for dog and cat food as we are for all religions and charities in the country!

These three "P's," Program, People, and Pocketbook, are all bound up in the pod of prayer. You have heard missionaries, both foreign and home, saying, "We can get along without your money, but we cannot get along without your prayers." In my days as an older adolescent, I used to say on hearing such a declaration, "That'll be the day; when they want our prayers more than they want our money!" But having visited numbers of our missionaries abroad and countless of our missionaries in the United States, I stand before you to declare again, "We need your prayers even more than we need your money!"

Yes, now is the time! Hopefully, you have understood why, and where, and how. If so, what can you do about it? Some of you need to respond by increasing your gifts to missions and to the Annie Armstrong Easter Offering and the foreign mission Lottie Moon Christmas Offering, as well as to the Cooperative Program. Others need to respond by considering the giving of their lives in service to the mission causes of the world. And all of us need to recommit ourselves to praying for the cause of missions for our nation and its rebellious lostness. And surely we need to pay for our missionaries who are striving, amid adversity, to present the good news to these people.

As we sing our hymn of invitation, "America the Beautiful," you will note that the hymnwriter asked God to bless our nation "from sea to shining sea." I urge you to give serious consideration that, "Now is the time for all good persons to come to the aid of their country." Will you come this morning?

Robert E. Bingham, Vice-president, Services
Home Mission Board

5
A Gift of Life
Volunteers Serve in Missions
David T. Bunch

And this, not as we expected, but first they gave themselves to the Lord and to us by the will of God (2 Cor. 8:5, RSV).

A "gift of life" best describes the people of God who serve as volunteers in missions. Our Lord is transforming lives through this selfless service.

Southern Baptists for generations have prayed for missions, have given millions of dollars to missions, and have sent their best young people into mission service. Pastors have preached that all can be missionaries—your opportunity, challenge, and calling. Suddenly laypersons believed what preachers proclaimed and began to ask, "Let us do mission work; let us serve where it will make a difference."

Giving of a Life

"Here we are—where do you want us to go?" inquired Houston and Cecile from Texas as they were welcomed to the Mission Service Corps orientation at Camp Copass, Denton, Texas. I was puzzled because they simply "showed up" without having sent an application. I inquired, "Where do you want to serve?" The Allens enthusiastically replied, "Where it makes a difference for one year." About a month later they packed their twenty-four-foot travel trailer and headed westward to Tucson, Arizona, to their assignment with the Baptist Friendship Center. Missionary Ross Hanna trained them to direct the satellite ministry in Nogales, Arizona. The Allens reminded missionary Hanna that they would be there only one year, to which he replied, "We will pray about that." Three months after the Allens arrived in Tucson, Bunch received a letter in which they wrote, "We worried about our house being unoccupied and the car sitting in the driveway deteriorating. We mentioned this to missionary Hanna. He said to pray about it. Within ten days a couple offered to buy our house. We closed the sale, stored our furniture, and drove our car here. Now we are in Nogales to do whatever Jesus has for us to do with no encumbrances. Our English literacy classes started this week. This is the most exciting thing we have ever done. We are here to stay." Houston and Cecile are making a difference. They are giving a gift of life.

America Needs the Gift of Life

I am concerned about home missions because I live here. I want America to be Christian. I want my neighbors to go to heaven. I want my friends to know about Jesus.

I see the great Northeast, the cradle of Baptists in America, now having almost a dearth of gospel preaching as Israel, the birthplace of Christ, is almost devoid of Christianity. I see the great cities ringed with thriving churches—some of which faithfully proclaim the gospel of Jesus. Yet, the once beautiful inner city now houses people who have little chance to hear the gospel. I see rural America, once a strong bastion of biblical proclamation, now in many areas, void of gospel preachers.

On one hand we have strong churches, effective preachers, multiplicity of multi-media communications saturating communities with the gospel. And we give thanks.

On the other hand, in America, we view communities of thousands without an evangelistic church, without an effective spiritual leadership, without voices of Christian communication, and without hands of Christian love.

You have directed our Home Mission Board to provide missionaries to permeate the untouched areas, to provide evangelists to proclaim the good news, and to provide persons to carry out the Christian ministry. This task we will take seriously!

We are committed to America. Why? Because America is a mission field. There are more lost people in Seattle, Washington, than Liberia, Africa; more in the city of Los Angeles than in Israel or Bolivia; more in Des Moines, Iowa, than in Grenada; more in St. Louis, Missouri, than in the Congo or Cyprus; and more in Dallas, Texas, than in Botswana.

There is a crisis in our land today—a crisis to preach the gospel of Jesus Christ because at least one-half of our citizens are lost, in need of Jesus.

Our Nation Awaits Your Gift

I am concerned about America—because America needs Christ. Evangelists, many of whom were lay preachers, crisscrossed America in the formative years. Their evangelism was so effective that in some counties one in two or three became Southern Baptists. Through their lineage we have grown to be the largest evangelical denomination in the U.S. Yet even with our strength—over one half of our population remains unaffiliated with any religion.

For centuries we sent missionaries to other lands—and we still must do so in increasing numbers—yet the nations have come to us by the millions. No longer is it strange to see commercial signs in languages other than English. No longer do we need to go to foreign lands to evangelize peoples of other races, creeds, and tongues. They are now in our communities. And most of them are awaiting our witness. The most recently established church nearest to the Home Mission Board in Atlanta, Georgia, is a Muslim mosque—a pagan temple!

If Southern Baptists had the same ratio of churches today as we had in 1889, we would start 15,000 churches now!

Chester and Willie Giddens did not impress me as urban church starters upon our first meeting. Chester stood head and shoulders above me, dressed in Western attire, and sporting expensive cowboy boots. The Lord had placed in their hearts a desire to start churches. Their activities include surveying to find interested persons, digging foundation trenches, nailing sheetrock, teaching boys and girls about Jesus, and helping lead Bible studies to develop embryo congregations. During these five years in the Mission Service Corps they have helped begin six church-type missions. Chester and Willie became concerned about our unreached nation and did something about it.

Your Gift as a Volunteer Missionary

You can pray and you can give so others can be active in missions, but home missions brings another confrontation to you—*participation.* Only to pray and give money for home missions, and not be a missionary in your own backyard and community, is abdicating Christian responsibility. Such is an injustice to the unsaved and mocks your commitment to Jesus Christ.

You have been faithful to pray. You have been faithful in tithes and special mission offerings like the Annie Armstrong Offering for Home Missions. Now God awaits your witness, *your* being a missionary.

About 50,000 persons answered "yes" to God's call to volunteer last year. They became missionaries for a week, a month, a season, or a year.

Bob and Bobbie took early retirement from the California public schools so they could be missionaries. Active in Sunday School, Church Training, WMU, and Baptist Men's work for years, they experienced a gnawing call "to go." As soon as early retirement was possible, they went to teach mission school in American Samoa. Teaching the principles of the faith as well as the ABC's, they, with the other three teachers, saw ten youth saved during classroom sessions.

Your Gift Is Tangible

The believers in the Macedonian churches inquired of the apostle Paul what he wanted. One wish was a generous offering for the persecuted saints in Jerusalem, but they surprised him by "first [giving] themselves."

It is appropriate to ask from this sermon, "What do you want from me?" As a believer I request three things for missions.

First, *consider going in a mission assignment for a year or two or if that is impossible, go for an extended vacation.* The needs are vast. The Foreign Mission Board reported that they had requests for over 10,000 volunteers in 1985. We at the Home Mission Board sent about 50,000 last year, and the needs are increasing. In my work with the Mission Service Corps, I have about ten requests for every volunteer, with 1,000 requests in the file today unfilled—no one to go. The requests include school teachers, preachers, construction workers, church musicians, WMU leaders, medical personnel, preschool

workers, church visitors, senior adult workers—whatever
your skill is, God has a place for it.

*Second, pray—pray for those who go, pray for yourself, pray for your
church, pray for persons who you know that are without Jesus as Savior.*
We have an Intercessory Prayer Line (1-800-554-PRAY) at
the Home Mission Board. Missionaries call in their prayer
needs, and Baptists call in to pray for these needs. We receive letters daily from the missionaries about God answering prayer.

One missionary requested prayer for property to con-
struct a church building. Within a few days, a woman
pledged to give the property. We rejoiced with him. A few
days later, he called again with the same request because the
initial property owner withdrew the offer. A few days later
he called again to report that another site had been found—a
much better one. "Pray without ceasing."

Third, *give.* Be faithful in your giving. Some give over and
above their regular tithes and offerings to help support a
volunteer missionary.

One layman, after reading about the needs of some volunteers, sent a $20,000 check to provide for their needs. A lady
on Social Security sent ten dollars and pledged a like amount
each month after reading the article in the September 1984
Royal Service magazine.

God is calling lay people to serve in missions. Our mission
leaders need them. A new state convention area called last
week. They need some funding help for a full-time Mission
Service Corps volunteer to do church music for two years,
Sunday School, and WMU leader training. The enlisted
volunteer has a master of religious education from seminary
and many years of experience. Another state seeks funds for
a volunteer to do state WMU leader work for two years.

Some of you have been given the "grace of giving." You
may activate this *gift* (talent) by helping God's called people

to go into mission service. Volunteers in missions become personal very quickly. You have the opportunity to go, to pray, and to give.

Giving All that I Am

The commitment to home missions is summed up in a letter which I received from Alleen in Washington state. She described how she and her husband were called to go from Oklahoma to Washington several years ago to teach school and help start Baptist missions. I thought, *Here is a real home missionary.* Then came the point of the letter, "I have $20,000 from insurance funds because of my husband's death. I want to use this so I can serve in missions. However, if you have someone who can go and do a better job than I can, I will give the money so they can go." We had a place with refugee ministries where Alleen served for three years.

The testimonies of volunteers in missions have verified the truth of the apostle Paul's words to the elders in Ephesus, "In all things I have shown you that by so toiling one must help the weak, remembering the words of the Lord Jesus, how he said, 'It is more blessed to give than receive' " (Acts 20:35, RSV).

David T. Bunch, Director
Mission Service Corps Coordination
Home Mission Board

6
The Challenge of Our Land
1 Corinthians 9:19-23

Joe Ford

The face of America is constantly changing, but the commitment of the Home Mission Board to present Christ to all our land has not changed. The goal to present the claims of Christ to our land is not something tacked onto our agenda that we may take or leave as we choose. It is our very purpose for existence. We believe to accept Christ as Lord is to enlist under the missionary banner. Thus, the missionary enterprise is the distinctive mark of being Christian.

As the apostle Paul outstretched his heart and his hands to embrace his area, so we too concentrate on every person to declare the liberation of Christ.

The Challenge of Concentrating on Every Person

Everyone is a special someone to Christ and to the Home Mission Board. We continuously affirm that God is no respecter of persons. We have no right to choose with whom we will share. We must not say we will concentrate on one kind of person and ignore another because they are different. All kinds of people are Jesus' kind of people and all must be ours. Today, the fields of America are white and black and brown, and red and yellow, awaiting the harvest. There are at least one hundred million Americans without Christ. We will not ignore or overlook anyone; we will be open and impartial toward all in making Christ known. We have the means, the message, and the mandate to reach *all* our land for Christ.

We understand that concentrating on every person also means concentrating on *all* the person. We are primarily concerned with the spiritual, but people are wholistic beings and cannot be compartmentalized. How can a Christian say, "I don't care if you're sick, I just want you to know if you're saved; I don't care if you're hungry, I just want to know if you're happy; I don't care if you've got a job, I just want to know if you've got the joy"? Though the spiritual emphasis is primary, the pathway to it is often paved with the cups of cold water given out in His name. In the New Testament there is no wedge driven between social action and evangelism. The Home Mission Board will not be a party to preaching the gospel but not practicing it. We refuse to pass out words instead of love.

God has led us, not to a special privilege, but to a special opportunity, to bring the good news to bear on every person. Therefore, we are challenged to cross over into every new frontier the changing face of America presents before us.

The Challenge of Crossing into Every New Frontier

If we are to enter today's frontiers with the good news there are some challenging, but not insurmountable, difficulties we face.

• *Geographical challenge*—Approximately 50 percent of our land lives in only fifty mega cities. Sixty-five percent of our churches are where only 2 percent of the population resides. We have been least effective in reaching people where most of America lives. The best way to increase our effectiveness is to increase our presence through new churches. We will continue to put high priority on congregationalizing. There will be other major efforts similar to Pentecost Sunday and

3,000 Mission Revivals in the future agenda of the Home Mission Board.

• *Language Frontiers*—The ethnic population of America is now approximately 134 million. Though the HMB has led in establishing congregations in nearly 100 language groups and over 1,600 of our missionary force are language missionaries, there are some 500 ethnic groups speaking 636 languages and dialects in America. The world has come to America, and we must make every effort for them to hear of Jesus, whether they remain or return to their native countries.

• *Physical Frontier*—Twenty-three million Americans are unable to adequately read or write; 15 million have impaired hearing; 1 3/4 million have visual impairment; 11 million have a drug addiction; and over two million older Americans suffer from acute loneliness. These are only a few of the many physical challenges we must effectively address to present Christ to our land.

• *Religious Frontiers*—Millions hide behind the cloak of cults and certain religious groups today. Pluralism can work against us when we confuse tolerance with compromising the gospel. Our people must be informed about the major gospel counterfeits of the twentieth century, as well as being effectively equipped to share personally the gospel through such efforts as CWT, LES (Lay Evangelism School), and Friendship Evangelism Seminars.

• *Cultural Frontiers*—America is a cultural menagerie. We must be as aggressive with those who love Bach and Beethoven as we are with those who love Willie Nelson and Kenny Rogers. We must be sharing the gospel in the arcade and the art gallery; the neighborhoods and the night spots; the ballet theater and the pool halls; the corporate suites and union offices; the management mecca and migrant camps.

Jesus made His world gasp at what He was willing to do

to reach people. The first-century disciples followed His example. Will we? We cannot afford to place restrictions on who deserves the gospel and strangle the umbilical cord of blessing which Baptists were founded upon.

Finally, the challenge of our land mandates that we commit every resource to proclaiming Christ.

The Challenge of Committing Every Resource

That commitment begins with me. How can I ask another to witness and minister if I do not? The credibility to extend the call to others depends upon my faithfulness. My primary responsibility for today's harvest field is not to plan for it, pray about it, give to it, *but to be in it.* Above all else, I am to lead by example.

In reaffirming my commitment I call upon you to do the same. Our greatest resource is our people. Whether you are a vocational minister, a bivocational minister, or a volunteer minister, the greatest contribution you can make to the cause of Christ is to be on mission wherever you live and in whatever you do.

At the Home Mission Board we fully understand that a professional missionary force is crucial to being effective, and we will continue to expand in size and strength. However, the professional missionary cannot begin to cover all the bases of need in our land. Therefore, we will major on equipping, according to the New Testament pattern.

Bold Mission Thrust is possible. "For with God, nothing shall be impossible" (Luke 1:37). As the weight lifter strains to his strength, so must the Southern Baptist Convention flex its muscles until it hurts. Jesus beckons us to stretch and sacrifice to our strength. This is no time to rest on past achievements and remain in the comfort zones of commitment.

In his later years, the great artist Renoir suffered from advanced rheumatism, particularly in his hands. When his good friend Matisse visited him, he could not ignore the fact that every brushstroke was causing Renoir great pain. Matisse asked, "Why is it that you still have to work? Why do you continue in such pain?" Renoir answered, "The pain passes, but the beauty remains forever."

It is time to enter the new vistas of victory in Jesus offered to all who believe. I look toward taking these next steps of victory in Jesus with you.

Joe Ford, Former Associate Vice-president
Home Mission Board, Evangelism

7

The Challenge Of Chaplaincy Ministries

Matthew 25:35-39

A. Carl Hart

I was hungry and you fed me, thirsty and you gave me a drink; I was a stranger and you received me in your homes, naked and you clothed me; I was sick and you took care of me, in prison and you visited me. The righteous will then answer him, "When, Lord, did we ever see you hungry and feed you, or thirsty and give you a drink? When did we ever see you a stranger and welcome you in our homes, or naked and clothe you? When did we ever see you sick or in prison, and visit you?" The King will reply, "I tell you, whenever you did this for one of the least important of these brothers of mine, you did it for me! (GNB).

Chaplaincy ministries is a unique approach to witnessing the gospel to people out of reach of the church. Today, more than 1,700 Southern Baptists serve in correctional institutions, hospitals, business, industries, military installations (around the world), mental health institutions, jails, motels, and other places. Chaplaincy ministries is an arm of the church, ministering where the church cannot. Chaplains are endorsed by the HMB.

A chaplain is a pastor, a teacher, a counselor, and a missionary equipped to minister to people in crisis, many times away from home or out of their normal walk of life. The chaplain's ministry, in most cases, is no different from that of a pastor, except that it will be in a different setting.

Southern Baptists can trace chaplaincy ministries back to the days of the Civil War, when a new challenge presented itself; to minister to service men who had left home to go to the battlefield. Again, this challenge came with World Wars I and II and the military involvement that followed. In the late '40s and '50s, chaplaincy began to spill over into civilian areas, and the challenge presents itself even more today.

Chaplaincy ministries today is pioneering a new breed of missionary, one who blends missions and ministry in the gospel pattern, touching lives in crisis, in the "crunch" moments, in the times of pain, suffering, loneliness, and hurt.

Chaplaincy has several characteristics that make it one of the most challenging ministries of our day.

Chaplaincy Is a Caring Ministry

The old saying, "Go see the chaplain and have your card punched," could be saying, "The chaplain is one who cares —go see him." Chaplains are caring persons. They spend their lives helping persons overcome circumstances that separate them from God. Chaplains, in a caring manner, apply the gospel to bring wholeness to persons broken by pressures, events, and conditions of our culture. Faced with prisoners in an institutional setting, the chaplain may have to exhibit "tough love," a cynical compassion that won't be conned, but will understand and forgive. Faced with workers battling marital or alcohol problems in an industrial setting, the chaplain may have to react with "selfless love," a sacrificial commitment that steps into the other person's shoes and identifies with the need before offering a solution. Faced with soldiers wounded and weary, the chaplain may have to share "angry love," an unrelenting devotion that battles the injustice as it binds the hurt.

In dozens of places, in hundreds of ways, faced with

human beings filled with frustration, anger, despair, rejection, the chaplain must offer "accepting love" which refuses to judge or condemn but readily welcomes, affirms, and expresses care.

While a chaplain made his rounds in a hospital one evening, he observed a young man in the waiting room for expectant fathers. The man was crying. The chaplain went over and expressed his concern and asked if there was anything he could do. The young man began telling the chaplain of his child that had been born with some physical problems. The chaplain prayed with him, then took him back into the intensive care unit where the man joined his wife and saw the child. The chaplain left his phone number with the man and encouraged him to call if he could be of help to the family. The chaplain visited the family daily while they were at the hospital.

When they went home, the chaplain encouraged them to call and keep him posted. Three weeks later, the man called and asked the chaplain to conduct the funeral for the baby. Several days after the funeral, the chaplain called to see how the man and woman were doing. As the young man answered the phone he said, "I was going to call you. Can you tell me of a church we can attend in this area?" The chaplain referred him to a church, then called the pastor and told him their story. The pastor immediately went to visit them. The couple made professions of faith that day and joined the church the following Sunday. It all started with a chaplain one night putting his hand on this young man's shoulder and asking, "Can I help you?" Chaplaincy is a caring ministry.

Thus, the word *chaplain* has established an image that can open doors for ministry. Often when those outside the church think of a "pastor" or a "missionary," they envision one who will attempt to change or convert a person to another belief. When they think of a "chaplain," however, they will often think of one who cares and wants to help.

Chaplaincy Is a Creative Ministry

Some years ago, we often heard about the role of the chaplain. Recently, though, little is being said because the role of one chaplain may vary greatly from that of another. Whether the chaplain serves in a children's hospital, a veterans' hospital, a general hospital, or a specialized hospital, one fact is certain: that chaplain must create his or her own ministry. No two institutions or military installations or correctional facilities have the same program format.

The chaplain creates a ministry that will relate to 300 boys in a juvenile institution while another chaplain has to formulate a ministry relating to 2,400 employees of an industry he or she may serve. The chaplain's creativity will determine a great deal of the success of his or her own ministry. I think of the chaplain that rotated ten boys each Sunday night, took them out of the youth institution, and to the park, where they grilled hot dogs and the chaplain taught them the parables. Later he encouraged eight laymen from a local church to help, and it became an effective outreach program of that church. I think of the chaplain who used his interest in art to gain the confidence of the hospital staff. He took art lessons and encouraged others to do the same. The hospital staff began talking to him about the patients, as well as themselves and their spiritual needs. But the chaplain first had to create something which would permit his acceptance as a professional person with a contribution to make to the healing process of the total person.

I am reminded of the military chaplain who had thirty backyard Bible studies in a military community in an attempt to minister to military families. I think of the industrial chaplain who rode with a driver of an eighteen-wheeler on his first run after an accident which involved a fatality. The chaplain testified "It was my way of saying I care." I think of the chaplain who formed small groups of youth offenders in an attempt to minister to their needs. He led them into giving themselves a name that described their needs. He then used music, art, research, and study to help them find out what really made them tick. He was able to confront them with the good news of Christ.

Whether a chaplain is serving in Saudi Arabia with an oil company or in south Georgia in a 100-bed hospital or on a military installation in Turkey or as an Air National Guard chaplain with an assignment in North Carolina, he or she will need to be creative. He or she must find a way to present the gospel, care for those that hurt, and listen to those who are lonely. It is not easy to be creative where the chaplain serves because he or she has to walk a narrow line. In industry, it may be that narrow line between management and labor. In a prison, it may be that narrow line between security/treatment staff and inmates; and in the military, it may be that narrow line between the officers and enlisted personnel. Regardless of which, overidentification with either could weaken the chaplain's ministry to all concerned.

Thus, chaplaincy ministries must become a creative approach to share the gospel with people where they are found.

Chaplaincy Continues to Be a Challenging Ministry

Chaplaincy has always been on the frontier of ministry. The traces of chaplains establishing mission churches in Europe, during and after World War II, are evident in many places. In the '50s and '60s, we saw hospitals as a frontier for ministry and under the training of those such as Wayne

Oates, Dick Young, and Myron Madden, they prepared themselves and met the challenge. Nine Southern Baptist chaplains serve as directors of chaplaincy for state departments of corrections (Florida, Texas, Georgia, South Carolina, Arizona, Arkansas, Virginia, Oklahoma, and Kentucky), and many of these are first-time positions. Chaplains have always been on the pioneering cutting edge. Chaplains were dealing with racial injustice in the '50s and '60s long before it hit the doors of our churches. They dealt with capital punishment, divorce, and other issues before the church faced up to these problems. Chaplains could not back away or sit down on these issues. They faced them and worked through them. These early struggles equipped the chaplaincy for the years ahead.

Chaplaincy has a bright future. The military chaplaincy is challenged with the continuing ministry to young troops who have sought the military to help them find out who they are and what they can do with their lives. Hospital chaplaincy is challenged to continue its training ministry for ministers desiring to help people in crisis. Chaplaincy is challenged to repeat its message over and over, which is: regeneration precedes rehabilitation. Business and industrial chaplaincy is challenged to minister to people who spend two-thirds of their waking hours in some kind of job, bringing with them their problems.

Chaplaincy will be challenged in the future to include more women in this ministry. The opportunities for women in chaplaincy are already growing rapidly and will increase in the years ahead. More and more women are going to prove their value in caring/counseling roles. As more and more women graduate from our seminaries, the challenge for women in chaplaincy will increase.

Volunteer chaplaincy has paved the way for many of our full-time chaplaincy positions. With this fact in mind, it will be interesting to see the number of full-time chaplaincy positions in the states of Florida and North Carolina that develop within the next ten years. Both of these states have started statewide emphases on volunteer chaplaincy. Other states, such as Texas, are initiating programs emphasizing this ministry.

About 1.8 million Americans now live overseas, not counting military personnel. That is an increase of 400,000 in the last five years. Chaplaincy, either through the Foreign Mission Board or the Home Mission Board, must feel the challenge to minister to these pockets of people around the world. The church will feel the challenge of chaplaincy in the future. Chaplains can move in and out of certain areas of the church community with freedom and welcome. His or her very title and skills carry this privilege. Thus, the church will be challenged to place a chaplain on the staff to relate to scores in the community who are institutionalized, hospitalized, confined, and hidden in secure apartments and business complexes.

The challenge of the chaplain continues to be directing people to the church where they can find love, God's Word taught, and a caring fellowship. Chaplaincy in the future will be a growing support to the local church.

Conclusion

Chaplaincy is taking the good news into situations where the traditional church is not represented, or where persons find it difficult to exercise their desire to worship. Many chaplains serve in situations where the church cannot, or will not, go. Some take the Word where denominations are denied entrance, such as military installations and the batt-lefield. Others use special skills and training to minister to unique persons, such as the mentally disabled.

Southern Baptist chaplains are missionaries who are a very vital part of the home mission force.

A. Carl Hart, Director
Chaplaincy Division
Home Mission Board

8

A Question of Adequacy

2 Corinthians 2:12—3:6

Robert L. Hamblin

Is it possible adequately to serve God in today's world? Some people would answer yes to this question. Others would reply no. Perhaps all people who respond in the affirmative would add some qualifications to their answer. Perhaps those who would say no would also qualify their answer. Most Christians would agree that service to God in today's world is most difficult. We probably would agree that we are inadequate for that service. However, when one looks at the needs of our world today, it is obvious that a Christian witness is needed. If we are not adequate to give that Christian witness, we must become adequate.

Our text is one of Paul's marvelous testimonies. The apostle was fond of giving his personal testimony about salvation. This text gives his personal testimony about a call to be a missionary evangelist. Paul was on his second missionary journey and had arrived in the city of Troas. It was his purpose to evangelize that city. However, he said that God opened a different door of opportunity for him. Paul stated that he had a vision in the night and "a certain man of Macedonia was standing and appealing to him, and saying, 'Come over to Macedonia and help us' " (Acts 16:9, NASB). Paul interpreted this as an open door of opportunity provided by the Lord. So he said, "I had no rest for my spirit, not finding Titus, my brother, but taking my leave of them I went to Macedonia" (2 Cor. 2:13, NASB). The call, which

Paul believed to be a call from God, was to come into Macedonia, a Greek province in the continent of Europe, to help
the people there. In verse 16, Paul asked, "Who is adequate
for these things?" (also see 3:5-6).

As Christians today face the challenge of the needs
around us, the same question comes to us. Am I adequate to
be a missionary and share the message of Jesus Christ with
the complex world in which I live? Our world is always
changing; we are constantly surrounded by challenges. Are
we adequate to meet those challenges? Every generation
faces its own fears, frustrations, changing life-styles, and
problems. It is difficult to interpret the gospel of Jesus Christ
to the generation in which we live. Our challenge in the
missionary endeavor is to evangelize. Our opportunity is to
invite the people of the world into a redemptive experience
with Jesus Christ, and to seek to bring them into the fellowship of believers, the body of Christ, the church. Who is
adequate to do this? Our society has so many facets that it
is complicated for the church to speak to its needs. But the
task of the church is still the same as it was in the day of
the apostle. The gospel must be taken to every lost person
in the world. I constantly find myself asking the question,
"Am I adequate to be a missionary and share the message of
Jesus with lost people?"

A Cry of Need

The vision of Paul was a very simple one. He saw a man
dressed in the clothes of Macedonians. He was pleading,
"Come over into Macedonia and help us." There is almost
a universal cry for help coming from every corner of our
society. Sometimes we are challenged by the statistics of our
changing world. Last year the 14 million-plus Southern Baptists won to Christ about 370,000 people. Thirty-five years

ago seven million Southern Baptists won to Christ about
335,000 people. America is growing. People are moving into
the cities of our nation. Our diverse culture is rapidly becoming more varied than ever before. Almost every language of the world is spoken in our land. Surely any person
who knows the grace of God can hear the cry of need.
Christians know that Jesus has the answer to that need. Paul
did go into Macedonia and he did help. There were many
physical needs that existed in Macedonia. People were hungry and they were sick. There was gross immorality and vile
hatred. The first place Paul entered in Macedonia was Philippi, where he encountered physical needs. When Paul
came to Philippi and began to meet people, he did not have
some set way to present the gospel to them, but he observed
their need and reacted to that need. He saw the good news
of Christ as good news for the whole person.

If Christians today answer with any degree of adequacy
the cry of need, we must not only obey the commission of
Christ to take the gospel to the world, but we must heed the
command of Christ to love our neighbor as we love ourselves. Jesus said to His disciples, "As the Father has sent me,
even so I send you" (John 20:21, RSV). When Paul saw a
young woman in Macedonia enslaved because of the physical greed of her masters, he brought the power of Jesus
Christ into her life, changing not only her spiritual condition, but also her physical condition.

Who is adequate to meet the needs of pain, hunger, dis-
tress, hatred, racism, and immorality? Jesus Christ is! So the
cry of need comes to us, and we do not answer in our own
power but in His power.

There was also a second need which was obvious. When
Paul heard the cry to come and help, there was a need within
him. He said, "I came to Troas for the gospel of Christ and
when a door was opened for me in the Lord, I had no rest

for my spirit, not finding Titus my brother, but taking leave
of them, I went to Macedonia" (vv. 12-13, NASB). The need
that existed in Paul's life was to be perfectly obedient to the
call of God. He was so glad to obey that call of God that he
did not even wait to find his friend Titus. He went immediately into Macedonia because he was constrained to do ex-
actly what God told him. Later Paul would write that his
purpose in responding to the call of God to evangelize was
his love for Christ. Christ had loved him and given Himself
for him. Paul's answer to that love was to love Christ. Out
of his love for Christ it was necessary for him to go into
Macedonia and do what God had called him to do.

You may feel inadequate to be a witness or to go into a
place other than your own home and share the message of
Christ, but as a child of God your love for Him compels you
to do it. There is not only a need in those who do not know
Christ, but there is also a profound need in those of us who
do know Christ. Our need is to share the love which we have
received from Jesus Christ.

A Covenant of the Needy

Our text indicates that God has created a covenant which
will answer the needs of mankind. Paul said, "But thanks be
to God who always leads us in His triumph in Christ, and
manifests through us the sweet aroma of the knowledge of
Him in every place. For we are a fragrance of Christ to God
among those who are being saved and among those who are
perishing; to the one, an aroma from death to death and to
the other, an aroma from life to life. And who is adequate
for these things?" (2 Cor. 2:14-16, NASB). Paul knew his
own inadequacy to share the gospel, but he also knew the
adequacy of Christ. He attested that he went into Macedonia, thanking God who leads us in His triumph in Christ.

Paul believed that Christ had triumphed over sin and all of its consequences by His own sacrifice on the cross. He wrote to the Colossians that Christ nailed our sins to the cross and openly triumphed over sin through His own sacrifice. God had not overlooked the needs of the Macedonians, but Christ had given Himself as a sacrifice for them that they might have life and victory. God has not overlooked the needs of the world. He cares about the hungering masses, about those who are torn in conflict and war, about the multitudes that are perishing in the immorality of their own guilt and sin.

He cares so much that He has loved each one. Out of that love His Son has died that we might be forgiven of our sins. It is no wonder that Paul would interpret his responsibility as delivering the sweet aroma of the knowledge of Christ in every place. It is good, even though it is difficult, to carry the message of Jesus to those who are perishing in sin. Notice that Paul calls it a two-sided aroma. It is the aroma of death to death, and to the believers the aroma of life to life. That is what makes it difficult. Many people of the world reject the message of Jesus Christ. They hear it as a condemning message because they refuse to receive Christ as Savior and Lord of their lives. Therefore, when they hear about Christ their hearts are pricked, they are reminded of their sins, and the message becomes one of death to death. But the wonderful aspect about the message is: it is a message of life to life to all who receive Jesus Christ as Savior and Lord.

Paul points out that because it is a message of life to life, it must be done with sincerity. The message must be presented as from God. Paul did not use cheap methods of evangelism. He says he did not "peddle" the Word of God, but he spoke in Christ and in the sight of God. Paul had surrendered his own life to Jesus Christ so he spoke of himself as "in Christ"; and he knew that what he was doing was being done in the power of Christ and, therefore, was witnessing as "in the sight of God."

It deserves our attention that Paul speaks of this covenant not only as a triumph, but also as something to be shared everywhere. God includes the entire population of the world in His love. Often the Bible speaks of God's love for the world. God wants every person everywhere to know Jesus Christ—those in the rural countrysides, those in the inner cities. It is God's desire to be all-inclusive. This makes the task even more difficult and causes us to cry out again, "Who is adequate for these days?"

Even though there is a covenant for the needy made by God, the task is still difficult. When Paul taught that the message brings life to life, that is wonderful, but when he said it brings death to death, that is a different matter. The messengers of Christ are often rejected because the world feels the sting of death in the Christian message. Paul's conclusion to this was: since he had received this ministry, he had also been the recipient of mercy from God, and therefore he would never lose heart. He indicated that if the gospel is veiled, it is veiled from the ones who perish because their eyes are blinded. He emphasized, "We do not preach ourselves, but we preach Christ Jesus as Lord" (2 Cor. 4:5, NASB). For God has said, "Light shall shine out of darkness" (v. 6). It is God's desire to save the lost, and He has made a covenant to do so. The Home Mission Board is committed to such a covenant.

A Conviction of Necessity

In the opening verses of chapter 3, Paul spoke of his responsibility as a necessity, not a necessity he had chosen for himself, but one God had given him. He assured the Corinthians that he was not condemning himself to them.

He neither needed to boast of himself nor did he need anyone else to write a letter to boast of him. He stated that the converted Corinthians, who were the recipients of his Macedonian ministry, were the evidences that God had been with him.

Paul answered the burning question that existed throughout his entire testimony: "Who is adequate for these things?" He wrote, "We are not adequate in ourselves to consider anything as coming from ourselves, but our adequacy is from God" (v. 5, NASB). Paul was stressing that he did not go to Macedonia in his own power, but he had gone in the power of God. So God was all-sufficient.

God is always all-sufficient. Our programs, ideas, and services may fail, but God never will.

The converted Corinthians had experienced something that man cannot do himself. Their hearts had been changed, and only God can do that. Paul concluded that he had confidence through Christ toward God. Christ did the work of salvation in the hearts of the believers.

I repeat: Paul confessed that he was not adequate in himself, but his adequacy came from God. God made him an adequate servant of the New Covenant.

The twofold conviction Paul had was that God had the power to save the Corinthians, and that God would use his life as a clear testimony to the lost.

We believers today need to share these necessary convictions. We must believe that Christ wants to save the lost and bless every person in the world with His presence. Christ is the light that shines out of darkness to give the light of the glory of God in the face of Christ to all people (see 2 Cor. 4:6).

You must believe that you are adequate in Christ to be used as a missionary who shares the word of God with those outside of Christ.

Who is adequate for these things? You are, if you commit yourself to Christ. Your adequacy is from God.

Robert L. Hamblin, Vice-president
Evangelism
Home Mission Board

9

Opportunity for Evangelism: Here Today, Gone Tomorrow
2 Corinthians 5:9-11

Richard H. Harris

We pray, preach, sing, and talk about "How We Love Jesus" and "How Great Thou Art," but we so rarely, if ever, tell the world. We have crosses everywhere, words of Bible verses and the name of Jesus inscribed on everything. Our talk is way ahead of our walk.

We have been given the Great Commission (Matt. 28:16-20). I believe if we are born again and love Jesus, as we say, we will want to share the message. As Christians, we have lost the vision of the transforming power of God in human hearts and lives (see 2 Cor. 5:17). From Washington down, we have been told what people need most is a better environment, more financial aid, and a better life-style. I'm for all of these but none can do for a person what the power of God can. People need a touch from heaven to answer that spiritual hunger for meaning, purpose, peace, and joy.

When we come to 2 Corinthians 5, Paul reminds us, in light of the certainty of death, that we need to take a good look at our lives and our commitment. We need to check our motivation for doing what we do. Paul calls us to remember that this this matter of being a Christian is serious, accountable business—and reminds us of our responsibilities as ambassadors for Christ.

Second Corinthians 5:9-11 is a somewhat debated passage as to meaning. Regardless of your interpretation as to whether there is one judgment or two, one fact is certain—

there shall be judgment! One of these days we are going to stand before the Lord and: "This was my life," and it will pass by. Right now God's "candid camera" is grinding away—every thought, word, deed, achievement, and motivation is being recorded. God is keeping watch—keeping record. Many Christians do not understand they must face this record.

I am not inferring that any *sin* which has been put under the blood of Jesus will be brought back. Praise God, "There is therefore no condemnation . . ." But no condemnation in salvation does not mean no accountability in sanctification. We must face the record of the deeds done in the body. We will be judged "according to [our works]," but not the person, not salvation (already judged).

Our Ambition in Life: Our Desire, Goal, Purpose (2 Cor. 5:9)

Paul wants every Christian to take a serious look at why he or she exists. In the King James Version, "Wherefore we labor," literally translated, is "wherefore we are ambitious." Paul is expressing his deep purpose in life. "Whether present or absent"—that is, whether out of the body or in the body, when the Lord called him to examination, he had a top priority. Paul wanted to be "accepted of Him" (Jesus) or literally to meet His approval.

Can you honestly say every deed, action, thought, etc., is done for one purpose—"to be accepted of Him"? How much has been done because we wanted to be accepted of a preacher, a church, friends, world, and the like? Nothing was more important to Paul than to please the Lord.

Have you ever really stopped to evaluate your life to determine your supreme ambition in life? Have you ever asked, "Why does our church exist?" Lots of members and preachers don't know from where the church has come, why it is here, and where it is going.

Fill in this statement: "For me to live is _____." Now be honest. Does your response really agree with your daily life? Just what is your ambition? Is it to be accepted of Him?

Our Appearance in Death: There Is a Summons and a Subpoena (2 Cor. 5:10)

Paul reminds us to evaluate our ambition in life because we are accountable in death. Paul anticipated a definite occasion when he would stand before the Lord to give account of his ambitions. Paul said *we must appear.* Where? The judgment seat of Christ to be judged. It is not a mere summons to appear, to show up, and have the roll checked. It is a servant before the king, a private before the general, everything being evaluated under a broad light.

The thought here is that we must *"all appear"* (author's italics) or "all must be displayed or manifested." The real danger today is a "So what?" attitude. This truth must not be taken lightly. We will appear before Christ to be judged. There will be no secrets in the closet, no hidden truths. Our secret sins will be public record, everything laid bare. An investigation will be conducted as to the deeds "done in [literally through] the body" (v. 10). One source reads, "Think about what His purposes and motives have been, and what he has accomplished."

The hymn writer says it clearly—"In my hand no price I bring, Simply to Thy cross I cling."

This passage is closely related to 1 Corinthians 3:11-15. Now have we built upon the foundation of the person and work of the Lord Jesus Christ? What have we done as builders for the King? Read 1 Corinthians 3:13.

Paul is talking about responsibility and accountability.

One day we will stand before the Lord and give account, "Lord this is the *talent* you gave me and this is what I have done; this is the *ability, personality, intellect, voice, teaching gift, money, influence,* etc., and here is what I did with it for you."

One day everything will be revealed for what it is. The *big* preachers, *important* church members, the *great* Christian witnesses, the great servants—it will take another word to confirm who these really are. "The Lord seeth not as man seeth; . . . but the Lord looketh on the heart" (1 Sam. 16:7, KJV).

The parable of the talents in Matthew 25:14-30 is a good illustration of the certainty of our accountability.

Our Appointment: Our Commission, Our Task

Evangelism is to missions what burning is to fire. From the *now in life* to the *then in death* Paul tells us in what direction we are to be moving and what should be our priority.

"Knowing therefore" or in light of what I have just said, in light of these truths we understand. We are to be ambitious about the right things because we are responsible. Now let's make it perfectly clear what we should be doing (2 Cor. 5:11a, 18,20). Paul mentioned: "persuade men," "reconcilers," "ambassadors." "Persuade men"—Paul was trying to convince the Corinthians that he was sincere about the right matters in life because he was aware God would hold him accountable. "Reconcilers"—for every person who has been brought into the right relationship with God, he or she has been given the responsibility of bringing others into a right relationship with God. Every Christian is to be a personal witness of what God has done for him/her. "Ambassadors" —God saves each believer and leaves him on this earth to be His spokesman, example (the representative) of Christ.

The opportunity of evangelism is at our door. Are we

taking advantage of it? Are we persuading? In 1981 Southern Baptists baptized 405,608, which was down about 5.6 percent compared to 1980. That figure equates a baptismal ratio of 35 to 1 if you count all Southern Baptist members and 24 to 1 if you just count resident members. This means, on the average, it took twenty-four resident member Southern Baptists one whole year to lead one person to Christ and bring that person to the baptismal waters of a Southern Baptist church. It doesn't appear we are taking our Lord's appointment very seriously. In 1982 there were 411,511 baptisms, which was up 1.5 percent compared to 1981. In 1983 there were 394,606 baptisms which was down about 4.1 percent. The baptisms-to-member ratio remained about thirty-five to one and twenty-four to one.

Again, last year over six thousand churches baptized no one! I realize many of these churches were without a pastor, but if we are taking our appointment seriously, the members should win one accidentally! Are we actually serious about Bold Mission Thrust and winning our world to Christ? The figures don't seem too encouraging.

The spiritual needs of humanity are the severest ever. How many lost people do you know? How many are you burdened for? Praying for? Witnessing to? Are there no unsaved people around us, no prospects? I go to church after church where they have identified few to no unsaved prospects by name. Few have a cultivative process of winning prospects to Christ.

Dr. O. B. Richardson, retired director of revival evangelism for the Baptist General Convention of Texas, tells the story of a young pastor who went to a small rural church. He was greeted by an old deacon who remarked, "Now, young man, I know that you are excited about winning our community, but we want you to know that we don't have many lost people.

"We have conducted several surveys, and we know for a fact that our small community has only four lost people. We are going to continue to try to win them, but they haven't given us much hope. We just want you to feed us on the Word and to help us have a good time in the Lord."

Dr. Richardson says that young pastor simply gave a single nod and proceeded with his enthusiasm to do what God had sent him there to do—to reach people for Christ and help them grow in grace and knowledge of the Lord Jesus (see 2 Pet. 3:18).

During the first six months of his ministry in that small community, the young pastor *baptized only seven of those four lost prospects!*

Friends, we have the most priceless treasure known to man. We can't find it anywhere else. Why aren't we talking the good news? Are people not interested? Are we afraid people won't hear?

In 1982, I attended a Colorado Evangelism Conference where a pastor testified that in the last six months he and his associate had knocked on about 3,500 doors. Only *one* person had been unkind or slammed the door in their faces, and that was to the associate just the day before. Don't think that everyone made a decision—they didn't. But the vast majority showed a definite "interest in spiritual matters." Our opportunity of evangelism is here today, but it may be gone tomorrow.

Let's tell it. Oh, how we need to be about our appointment. If serving Jesus is worth anything, it's worth everything. For every "Come unto me" in the Bible, there is a "Go ye therefore."

    Jesus saves, Jesus saves
      Waft it on the rolling tide:
    Jesus saves! Jesus saves!

Tell to sinners far and wide:
Jesus saves! Jesus saves!
—Priscilla Owens

If we ever start practicing what we preach, we will realize how we need continually to evaluate our *ambition* because we know there will be an *appearance* before Christ to give account. We will take our *appointment* seriously, and we will daily be about the task of winning our world to Jesus Christ. Our opportunity of evangelism is here now, but it may be gone tomorrow!

Richard H. Harris, Director
Mass Evangelism Department
Home Mission Board

10
Why the Church?
Acts 1:1-9

Leonard G. Irwin

The two cardinal events highlighted in the New Testament after the crucifixion of Christ are His resurrection and the gift of the Holy Spirit at Pentecost.

It is essential that the church in any age continue to magnify these two glorious events, because the very survival of the church depends upon their emphasis. The resurrection of our Lord is the church's assurance of victory—a victory, not only over the sting of death, but also over the blight of sin. Our Master never intended His church to be passive but to be agressive and assertive. In speaking to His disciples in Caesarea Phillipi, Jesus issued a command of aggression when He pronounced, "Upon this rock I will build my church, and the gates of hell shall not prevail against it" (Matt. 16:18). When the church moves out boldly, even the stronghold of sin cannot resist its thrust.

The gift of the Holy Spirit at Pentecost is the assurance of power—a power not only over temptation for survival, but a power for bold, sacrificial service in His kingdom.

There is another meaningful event in a middle position between these two foundational experiences and has an important place in the life and role of the church. The event is the ascension of our Lord. In these last words of Christ to His disciples the church finds its reason for being.

The most explicit description of the ascension is found in Acts 1:6-9, "When they therefore were come together, they asked of him saying, Lord, wilt thou at this time restore again the kingdom to Israel? And he said unto them, It is not for you to know the times or the seasons, which the Father hath put in his own power. But ye shall receive power, after that the Holy Ghost is come upon you: and ye shall be witnesses unto me both in Jerusalem, and in all Judaea, and in Samaria, and unto the uttermost part of the earth. And when he had spoken these things, while they beheld, he was taken up; and a cloud received him out of their sight."

As the disciples moved up the mountain that day with Jesus, I am sure there were many burning questions in their hearts about the future and their place in the world after His departure. Yet, one question took precedence over all others; it was the question Israel had asked for centuries, "Lord, wilt thou at this time restore again the kingdom to Israel?" There must have been a brief silence after the question, the Lord looking into the eyes of those who had been most faithful to Him. The disciples were riveted to their positions, awaiting the proclamation of the restoration.

However, Jesus did not answer their question but corrected it and, in so doing, shifted the emphasis which is the pivotal point in the redemptive program of God. "But ye shall receive power, after that the Holy Ghost is come upon you: and ye shall be witnesses unto me both in Jerusalem, and in all Judaea, and in Samaria, and unto the uttermost part of the earth."

A Universal Kingdom of God

Jesus shifted the emphasis from a one-nation kingdom of one people to a universal kingdom of God for all mankind. The kingdom would not be for Israel alone but for Judea, Samaria, and on to the uttermost part of the earth. Jesus taught that His church is for everyone—"red and yellow, black and white, they are precious in His sight."

This little group of faithful followers Jesus was leaving behind to carry out His great redemptive program, and yet changes were needed in the hearts of these disciples. They were men of narrow vision and deep-seated prejudice. He envisioned the church as a fellowship of all people; their vision was of a kingdom for Israel alone.

Although Jesus used geographical terms in stating His commission to the church, the implications were deeper than mere places on a map. The church must understand that the love of God encompasses all the kingdoms and people of this world.

One of the most immediate challenges Southern Baptists face in reaching this nation for Christ is effectively sharing the gospel with a society that is highly pluralistic. Our nation is made up of some 230-million-plus people and 119 million of these are identified as belonging to an ethnic/language-culture group other than our national culture.

God has seen fit to bring the world to our door. How are we as Southern Baptists, the strongest evangelical denomination in the land, going to respond? We are responding, that is true, but are we moving with the rapidity that the situation demands? The largest program budget of your Home Mission Board is the language missions budget. Southern Baptists in our nation each Sunday worship in some eighty different languages. Studies indicate we are starting at least 350 language-culture units annually. But is this enough?

The critical needs are for leadership and literature. There are well over one thousand Southern Baptist language units without a leader, and we have just begun to provide only in a few languages the literature essential to the growth and effectiveness of the ethnic church.

To meet this challenge God has placed before us will require, not only that we understand the changing mosaic of our nation's population, but that we also recognize our individual, personal responsibility in reaching these millions for the Master.

A Transforming Spirit

Jesus also shifted the emphasis from the restoration of the past to the transformation of the present. He moved the focus from the restoration of a mundane kingdom to "ye shall receive power," a dynamic, transforming force for the present. The disciples were looking back through centuries of history to David and his time of glory. Jesus was looking at a lost and helpless world in His day and was saying that this world can be transformed, not into an ancient kingdom of yesterday, but into the glorious kingdom of God.

We must never forget our past as Southern Baptists. We have a rich heritage as God has molded and shaped us for this very hour. But we know that yesterday's victories alone will not provide the power for tomorrow's challenges. We must accept the mandate from our Lord to move forward with the transforming power of the Holy Spirit.

As we study the Book of Acts we see this power, not only radically transforming lives, but also the structure of the fellowship of faith. It was the Holy Spirit as a transforming and enabling force which provided the mission imperative and called men and women to a world mission task in the early church. Dr. John Bunn states, "At Pentecost the mighty acts of God's power sealed in the minds of the converts, and those established in the faith, that the power imparted by the Spirit was not only dependable and reliable but incapable of failure."[1]

There is no greater illustration in the Bible of the trans-

forming power of the Holy Spirit than that of the early
disciples. Their vision was narrow and fraught with prejudice in the last hour with Jesus, but their hearts and minds
were transformed after the experience at Pentecost. As
Harry R. Boer notes, "It is clear that once the intent of the
Spirit became clear to the church she hurdled the national
and racial barriers and sent the gospel even during the life-
time of the first generation of Christians to the limits of the
empire."[2]

Not only is the transforming power of the Holy Spirit
needed today to change the lives of those who know Him
not, but we as Southern Baptists need the transforming energy in our churches if the goal of Bold Mission Thrust is to
be accomplished by the year AD 2000.

Southern Baptists have the strength in numbers, 36,000-
plus churches and some fourteen million-plus members, but
do we have the commitment to permit the Spirit's transforming power to act in us and through us?

There are signs that the Spirit is working in our churches.
We have more people involved in missions today than at
any time in our history. We have some seven thousand-plus
career missionaries and thousands of others who have
become personally involved, if only for a short period of
time, in both our foreign and home mission strategies and
programs.

There are indications that Southern Baptists are becoming
more aware that reaching this land and our world for Christ
must begin with the supportive power of prayer. We have
always talked about prayer, but it seems that today, prayer
is practiced in the lives of our people with deeper intensity.

There is a spirit of expectancy among Southern Baptists
in this decade that was not there in the sixties and early
seventies, a renewed hope which has brought about a new
vision and a new commitment in the lives of many.

While we give thanks for these and other manifestations of the transforming power of the Holy Spirit, we as His people must be willing to follow Him in more fervent commitment and concern.

To Be a Witness

Jesus also shifted the emphasis from a speculation of the future to a demonstration in the present.

Jesus promised, "Ye shall be witnesses unto me." As planners, we must always look into the future so we can capitalize on the opportunities of tomorrow and avoid the pitfalls of the unknown. On the other hand, we must not sacrifice our present witness for future speculation. The church is to demonstrate the redeeming and transforming power of God's love to every generation.

Jesus actually said, "Ye shall be my witnesses." Note that Jesus did not say, "Ye shall witness to me," but "Ye shall be my witnesses." The use of the verb "to be" must be understood in its literal sense. The expression carries with it more than what the church should do; it states emphatically what the church should be. The church exists for witnessing—not just part of the redeemed, but all born-again children of God are to be witnesses.

An excellent illustration of the victory that can come to a church when this imperative is prayerfully carried out is found in the second chapter of Acts. When the little band of 120 faithful followers gave witness to the saving power of Jesus Christ, 3,000 redeemed souls were added to the church.

We, as Southern Baptists, must confess our neglect of this imperative to be witnesses. One fact indicating our ineffectiveness is that our churches baptize an average of one person for approximately every thirty-six members, or even worse.

While recognizing that numbers are not the only indicator of an effective witness, we must conclude that we are not the witnesses our Lord envisioned His church to be. It is true that we will never accomplish our Bold Mission Thrust objective in our nation without a more serious commitment to being what Christ commanded us to be.

Because witnessing is not an alternative but an imperative for the church, priority must be given to equipping the members to carry out this commandment. For the past three years there has been an encouraging growth of concern in our churches for personal witness training.

The overwhelming response to the 1986 simultaneous revivals, "Good News America, God Loves You," attests to the concern of Southern Baptists to do the Master's will.

Another hopeful sign that Southern Baptists are taking seriously this imperative is the excellent response of the churches in starting new work. One is made keenly aware, as one studies the Book of Acts, the important role that church planting had in the spreading of the gospel.

Dr. Penrose St. Amant, in writing of Paul's strategy for establishing churches, explained, "Paul understood the elemental fact that the gospel, once planted, would spread by its own intrinsic power."[3]

In the establishing of churches, the gospel is not just shared to one generation, but there is a continuous witness for many generations to come. The established church is not only a witness to the community but also a fellowship to the redeemed. Through this fellowship one is strengthened in God's Word, one's faith in a loving God, and one's sincere efforts to be a witness.

Jesus, standing with the disciples He loved so dearly, realized that the church He willed it to be was a revolutionary concept and even beyond comprehension for those He was leaving behind. Yet, He knew that Pentecost would bring a new understanding, a new hope, and a new vision to that small band of faithful followers.

The Book of Acts is a testimony to the effectiveness of the church when the spiritual resources available to the church are permitted to work in the lives of God's people. In one generation the gospel spread to the far corners of the Roman empire.

The marvelous truth is that this same love, this same power, this same victory can be ours as we share the good news of the gospel with our generation. If we fail, the failure will come from our lack of concern and commitment. Because Christ is the same yesterday, today, and forever, He is ready to bless and bring victory to His church in every generation.

Why the church? Jesus proclaimed, "Ye shall be my witnesses." The world is yours, the power is yours. The question that each must answer is, "Am I His to be used by Him for His glory?"

Leonard G. Irwin, Vice-president
Planning
Home Mission Board

NOTES
1. Morris Ashcraft, *Mission Unlimited* (Nashville: The Stewardship Commission of the Southern Baptist Convention, 1976), p. 228.
2. Harry R. Boer, *Pentecost and Missions* (Grand Rapids: Wm. B. Eerdmans Publishing Company, n. d.), p. 130.
3. Ashcraft, Ibid., p. 139.

11

We Cannot Leave Our Brother Behind

Gen. 43:1-5

Emmanuel L. McCall

The famine in Canaan got worse, and when the family of Jacob had eaten all the grain which had been brought from Egypt, Jacob said to his sons, "Go back and buy a little food for us."

Judah said to him, "The man sternly warned us that we would not be admitted to his presence unless we had our brother with us. If you are willing to send our brother with us, we will go and buy food for you. If you are not willing, we will not go, because the man told us we would not be admitted to his presence unless our brother was with us" (Gen. 43:1-5, GNB).

The story of Joseph in Egypt really begins when Jacob (Joseph's father) arrives at his Uncle Laban's home in Haran and falls in love with Rachel. When he asks permission to marry her, Laban reminds Jacob that a dowry is always required as part of a marriage transaction. In his haste to flee from his brother Esau's wrath, Jacob has brought no possessions with him. If Jacob will agree to work for seven years, however, Laban will compute those wages as sufficient dowry.

The seven years pass by swiftly for Jacob. But Laban deceives Jacob on the wedding night by giving him Leah, Rachel's older sister. Confronted with Jacob's anger at being deceived, Laban offers Rachel on the condition that Jacob will give Leah the benefit of the honeymoon week and agree to work seven more years.

So Jacob is stuck with a difficult situation. He has a wife whom he loves (Rachel) and who knows she is loved. He also has Leah, who is not loved, and who knows she is not loved. A contest is on between the two women to win Jacob's favor.

Leah is fortunate. She bears children, hoping thereby to earn Jacob's love. In the early years of the marriage Rachel is unable to bear children, so she resorts to a cultural custom: she gives Jacob her personal maid Bilhah so he can father a child by her.

Leah, although still bearing children, does not want to be outdone. She gives Jacob her personal maid Zilpah so that she, too, can bear children for her.

Later, Rachel is able to have children and gives birth to the last two born to this tangle of relationships. The tally reads: Leah—six sons, one daughter; Bilhah—two sons; Zilpah—two sons; Rachel—two sons.

Jacob now has four women, but he loves only one. He has thirteen children, but loves only two: Joseph and Benjamin. The favoritism in that household undoubtedly causes constant tension, anger, and jealousies. Those who know they are not loved despise those who are loved. Those who are loved behave arrogantly toward the others.

People who are not loved have noticeably different perspectives on life from those who are supported by love. Children produced by unloving parents come into the world handicapped. Parents who show favoritism among their children set themselves up for conflict, competition, anger, and hatred. So it is with Jacob.

Jacob shows favoritism. Even though he is the eleventh child, Joseph is assumed to be his father's heir. Jacob sees in Joseph an opportunity to achieve his unfulfilled ambitions.

The boy is adorned with a "coat of many colors" (some versions call it a "robe with full [or long] sleeves"). He stays at home to listen to and be schooled by elite visitors. While the others work in the scorching sun, eating coarse food and wearing plain clothing, Joseph enjoys fine food, good wine, and stylish garments.

To make matters worse, he tells his brothers of a dream he has had: they were in the fields tying up wheat, and the brothers' sheaves bowed down to his.

The breaking point comes when he tells of a dream in which the sun, moon, and stars bowed down to him. His brothers are tired of this pampered brat's arrogance, his favored treatment, and his constant reporting of their activities to Jacob.

Joseph is often portrayed as the one greatly sinned against —the ideal son possessed of a restless imagination. Let's be honest in admitting that Joseph after being sold into slavery is different from the Joseph who strutted before his brethren. For God to use him Joseph has to be humbled.

The humbling experiences begin when Joseph is stripped of his fine garments, placed in a dry well to die, and sold as a slave. His brothers dip his clothing in goat's blood, carry them to Jacob, and let him believe a wild animal has devoured Joseph. Jacob recovers from his grief only when Joseph is discovered as ruler in Egypt many years later.

Even after Joseph's rise from an outside slave to house servant, to the household manager and back to the dungeon because of his master's wife's attempted seduction, the humbling experiences continue. Joseph has long hours to remember his arrogant provocation of his brothers. He has time to be disciplined by the Spirit of God so he can make the unique contribution God has destined for him.

In our moments of honesty, each of us can recall experiences that humbled us, reduced our cockiness, and made us more usable in God's service. Like the refiner's fire that exposes the impurities in gold, God is constantly at work to bring out the best in us. So it is with Joseph.

The refined Joseph possesses qualities which any of us should desire. He becomes a champion of human fairness. He develops superior inner strength, with a sense of honor and a mindfulness of God. While he could have used Potiphar's wife for sexual gratification and his political advantage, he refused to let personal desires or selfish ambition betray his integrity.

The evidence that God rewards faithfulness is seen in Joseph's last imprisonment. The Pharaoh's former wine steward and chief baker are also imprisoned. Each is disturbed by dreams. Joseph uses his God-given ability to solve the riddle of those dreams. When he interprets the wine steward's dream Joseph says, "Please remember me when everything is going well for you, and please be kind enough to mention me to the king and help me get out of this prison" (Gen. 40:14, GNB).

The wine steward's moment of truth comes two years later when the Pharaoh has disturbing dreams. In one of them, seven fat cows come up out of the Nile River and begin to eat grass. Later seven skinny and bony cows come up and eat the fat cows. In another dream seven heads of full grain are devoured by seven thin ones. The Pharaoh is disturbed because his dream interpreters, wise men, and magicians cannot solve the riddles. The hand of God is at work: He gives the interpretation only to his chosen servant, Joseph. The wine steward, who had forgotten his pledge to Joseph, now remembers him.

Joseph is released from prison, not just because he can interpret dreams, but because he prescribes wise courses of action. He is placed second in command of the nation and given the king's signet ring, the symbol of royal authority. Only the Pharaoh is superior to him.

To prepare for the seven years of famine that will follow seven years of plenty, grainaries must be built and supplied. The best agricultural techniques must be put to work. No idleness will be countenanced.

The famine reaches Canaan where Joseph's family are roving nomads. Jacob hears that there is food in Egypt and sends ten of his sons to buy grain. Only the last son, Benjamin, remains at home. Jacob has surrounded Benjamin with protective care after his hopes were dashed by the reported death of Joseph. Benjamin is the only remaining son born to a loving relationship with Rachel. If anything happens to him, Jacob would give up and die.

Divine providence brings Joseph's brothers to the area where Joseph is supervising sales to foreign customers. Recognizing his brothers, Joseph remembers his childhood dreams of sheaves of grain bowing down to his, and the sun, moon, and stars doing homage. But he cannot reveal himself yet. Intrigue intensifies the story. Joseph accuses the men of spying. In the verbal exchange he learns that Jacob is still alive and Benjamin is with him. Joseph knows that the only way to get Jacob and all of the family into his protective custody in Egypt is to maneuver a way to get Banjamin there. His bargain is that one of the men, Simeon, must stay while the others return to Canaan. The imprisoned man can be ransomed only by the bringing of Benjamin.

During his conversation with his brothers, Joseph turns aside to cry because of the flood of emotions that overwhelm him. He hears Reuben scold his younger brothers by suggesting that this recent misfortune is God's judgment on their wickedness toward young Joseph. Even though he has been in Egypt a long time, Joseph has not forgotten the

Hebrew language. He speaks to his brothers through an interpreter, although he understands every word they say.

The story moves to yet higher levels of suspense. Joseph orders his brothers' sacks to be filled with grain—and that each man's money be put back in his sack. When one of the men opens a sack on the way home and finds his money, fear of reprisal grips the brothers. The fear turns to dread when they arrive home and every one of them finds his bag of money.

As expected, Jacob refuses even to consider giving up Benjamin, as demanded by the Egyptian governor in exchange for Simeon. He is resolute about not giving in. But the famine changes that. When the family has exhausted its food supply, Jacob asks his sons to go back to Egypt.

Judah reminds Jacob that they have to take Benjamin. Judah says to him: "The man sternly warned us that we would not be admitted to his presence unless we had our brother with us. If you are willing to send our brother with us, we will go and buy food for you. If you are not willing, we will not go, because the man told us we would not be admitted to his presence unless our brother was with us" (Gen. 43:3-5, GNB).

Let me leave the story momentarily to do a bit of sermonizing. No one can honestly claim to be self-made, self-sufficient, and independent of others. Anyone who has anything to boast about has been helped along by parents, family, friends, associates, supporters, and even strangers.

Those who feel they have achieved must remember those who are left behind, those who have not achieved. They are not necessarily lazy or incompetent. In most instances they have lacked supportive opportunities. Some are handicapped because they have no models. Some have no one to inspire them or provide incentives. Some have to struggle

just to survive. They have no energy to move beyond existing. *We cannot leave our brothers behind.*

In this age when exact skills are needed in order to be
employed, we who possess certain skills must find ways to
equip others. *We cannot leave our brothers behind.*

Today when many are seeking hope by shooting up dope,
you and I must be used of God to declare, "There is a better
way." *We cannot leave our brothers behind.*

Our jails are full of young people needing direction, purpose, and somebody to love them. We on the outside must
never let snobbish arrogance cause us to feel we are above
them. *We cannot leave our brothers behind.*

Senior adults are struggling to survive on fixed incomes.
The later years that ought to be filled with contentment are
often full of loneliness and despair. *We cannot leave our brothers
behind.*

Children born to single-parented families need someone
to help them become well-rounded and reach their highest
potential. *We cannot leave our brothers behind.*

Some people do not know that God loves them and cares
about their welfare. Those of us who are saved cannot be
complacent while people need to hear the Good News. *We
cannot leave our brothers behind.*

When we stand before the Righteous Judge He will not
ask about the honors and recognitions we have received. He
will not be concerned about what positions of authority we
have held. He will not ask how much we attended church
or how much we gave. He will only want to know about
where we left our brothers.

"Then the King will say to the people on his right, 'Come,
you that are blessed by my Father! Come and possess the
kingdom which has been prepared for you ever since the
creation of the world. I was hungry and you fed me, thirsty
and you gave me a drink; I was a stranger and you received

me in your homes, naked and you clothed me; I was sick and you took care of me, in prison and you visited me.' The righteous will then answer him, 'When, Lord, did we ever see you hungry and feed you, or thirsty and give you a drink? When did we ever see you a stranger and welcome you in our homes, or naked and clothe you? When did we ever see you sick or in prison, and visit you?' The King will reply, 'I tell you, whenever you did this for one of the least important of these brothers of mine, you did it for me!' " (Matt. 25:34-40, GNB).

Thank God, Jacob's sons do not leave Benjamin behind. With fear and trepidation they journey to Egypt, bringing the money that had been returned on the first trip, plus enough for the anticipated purchases. They bring gifts with which to appease the Egyptian governor should it become necessary.

God has already been at work in Joseph's heart. Joseph has no intention of leaving his brothers behind. In the fulfillment of God's time Joseph tells them who he is.

Joseph does not leave his brothers behind in forgiveness. He gives a higher interpretation to their deed of hate. "Now do not be upset or blame yourselves because you sold me here. It was really God who sent me ahead of you to save people's lives" (Gen. 45:5, GNB).

Joseph does not leave his brothers behind in love and care. He asks them to bring their families to Egypt and live in the choice land of Goshen. Famine can no longer touch them since they are now in a land of plenty. His political influence is not kept for himself and his immediate family. He sees to it that all of his brothers have what they need.

Joseph does not leave his brothers behind in participation in God's redemptive acts. In Egypt, God develops a people to be His elect, His chosen, a royal priesthood, a holy nation, prepared to extol the praises of Him who brought them out of darkness and into His marvelous light.

God is still asking: Where is your brother? God is still visiting humankind, desiring to be in loving fellowship. While He could enlist whatever measures He wishes to bring all men to Him, God gives us the opportunity of joining Him in His purposes. *We cannot leave our brothers behind!*

Emmanuel L. McCall, Director
Black Church Relations Department
Home Mission Board

12

The Mizpah in New Testament Perspective

Genesis 31:49

Emmanuel L. McCall

The Lord watch between me and thee while we are absent one from another (Gen. 31:49, KJV).

May the Lord keep an eye on us while we are separated from each other (Gen. 31:49, GNB).

I was breast-fed on the Mizpah. In the church of my youth every service concluded with a recitation of: "May the Lord watch between me and thee while we are absent one from another. This we pray in Jesus' name. Amen." The second sentence is not a part of the original Mizpah but was added to give Christian respectability.

When I say "every service concluded with a recitation of the Mizpah," I do mean *every* service: Sunday School classes, Sunday School assembly, morning worship, each mission organization, the prayer band, Sunday evening services, choir rehearsals, midweek prayer services, teachers' meetings, *every service.* Since my family was totally involved in the life of the church, we children had to go to everything.

When I went to Louisville for college, I discovered that the Kentucky churches did not recite the Mizpah. Instead they had a closing prayer or benediction. At first I was surprised, then concerned, for the Mizpah had seemed such a spiritual thing to say. I interpreted it to mean that the fellowship and love of Christians was so great that they wanted the Lord to watch over one another when they were absent from one another. I was sure that as we recited it in Valley Baptist Church in Wheatland, Pennsylvania, we did so with abiding affection, love, and concern. I later discovered that some of those who spoke the Mizpah hated one another, plotted, schemed, lied, and did all of the other things that church people sometimes do.

It wasn't until my seminary years that I discovered the original intent of the Mizpah. It had nothing to do with fellowship, Christian love, or trust. It was just the opposite. The Mizpah was for Jacob and Laban an oath to keep them from destroying each other. Let's look at the record.

After Jacob had succeeded in tricking his brother Esau out of both the birthright and the blessing, he had to flee for his life. Instructed by his mother, Rebecca, he fled north to the home of his uncle, Laban. There he fell madly in love with Rachel, one of Laban's daughters. When he approached Uncle Laban about his desire to marry Rachel, the essence of the reply was, "Now Jacob, you have no dowry. You left home in such a hurry that you brought nothing with you. I just can't *give* my daughter away. But I tell you what I'll do: if you work for me for seven years, I'll consider what you would have earned as sufficient dowry. At the end of that time you may marry Rachel." So eager was Jacob to please Laban and win Rachel that he worked hard those seven years. Time moved so swiftly that it "seemed like only a few days to him, because he loved her" (Gen. 29:20, GNB).

But on the wedding night, after seven years of anticipation, Uncle Laban pulled a trick on Jacob. The wedding was held at night by oil lamps. The bride was adorned in a heavy black veil. Jacob did not know that the woman with whom he spent the wedding night was not Rachel, but her older sister Leah.

When confronted with his deed, Laban reminded Jacob that the custom was that the oldest daughter married before her younger sisters. Although Leah is described as having tender (or "lovely," v. 17, GNB) eyes, she was not as beautiful as Rachel. Laban had to marry Leah off.

He was ready with a new proposal to Jacob. "Wait until the week's marriage celebrations are over, and I will give you Rachel, if you will work for me another seven years" (v. 27, GNB).

When Jacob completed the fourteen years, he had yet other problems. In addition to the two wives, Jacob also had his wives' handmaids who bore him children. These four women had borne him eleven sons and one daughter. But he was still dependent on Laban.

Jacob's own shrewdness and Laban's greed resolved that problem. Jacob had been a successful herdsman, developing Laban's flocks so they grew tremendously. Jacob pretended to want to leave as a way of getting Laban to ask him to stay. Jacob proposed that he would keep the speckled, spotted, brown, and black sheep and goats as his wages. Since few animals bore these colors, Laban assumed he had a good bargain. To assure his conniving, Laban had his son remove the male goats with spots or stripes and the females that were speckled or spotted. He removed all of the black sheep. These were separated from the rest of the herd the distance that could be traveled in three days.

Seeing that he had been tricked, Jacob resorted to a scheme of his own. He took branches from poplar, almond and plane trees, and stripped some of the bark so that the branches had white stripes. Since the animals mated at the water troughs these branches were placed there only when healthy animals watered. The end result was that most of the offspring for the next six years were striped, spotted, and black sheep and goats. Laban's newer flock of white sheep and goats were weak and few.

As Jacob's fortunes increased, Laban's sons saw their father's flocks diminish. Their heritage and fortune were in jeopardy. Sensing that a showdown was imminent, Jacob waited until Laban and his sons had gone to shear their sheep, gathered his family and possessions, and began the trek back to Canaan.

When word reached Laban about what Jacob had done, he first returned home to secure his household gods—idols that would protect him in his battle with Jacob. He did not know that Rachel, anticipating her father's actions, had taken the idols and put them in the saddlebag of her camel.

Laban and his men caught up with Jacob seven days later. Both men were afraid of the other, knowing that each was a master at deception. Jacob was outnumbered by armed strength. Laban was handicapped without the idols that gave him assurance in battle. Jacob accused Laban of all the trickery he had done. Laban reminded him of the deceptions he (Jacob) had perpetrated. Two masters of deceit faced each other. What could be done to resolve the crisis?

If Jacob harmed Laban, his wives would never forgive him of the death of their father. If Laban harmed Jacob, his daughters would never forgive him for the loss of their husband. What could these two cowards do? They did what cowards often do. They tried to place the responsibility on a third entity. This time it was God whom they tried to make responsible.

They gathered stones and made a memorial marker. As a sign of covenant they ate a meal at the marker and made an agreement. The agreement was that Laban would not come south of that marker to harm Jacob, and Jacob would not go north of the marker to harm Laban. They each now had assigned territories. They asked the Lord to stand guard at the marker to be sure neither of them would break the agreement. Thus, two con artists tried to reduce the Lord to a sentinel. This is the Mizpah.

Obviously this Mizpah does not represent New Testament fellowship or Christian concern. Laban and Jacob had a utilitarian concept of God. They saw him as a God to be manipulated, one who would aid them in their devious ways.

New Testament perspectives of fellowship demand that we recognize God as our Father, to whom we are all subject, Jesus Christ as our brother, by whom we are all judged, and the Holy Spirit as our empowerment, through whom we move toward divine likeness.

New Testament perspectives also demand that any conduct which reduces our brothers and sisters to objects of our gratification is unworthy of those who claim to follow Christ. Over and over again the New Testament admonishes us to be disciplined in love, compassionate and considerate of others, to work for the welfare and good of others, and to reflect the mind and spirit of our Lord.

In spite of what we know about the background of the Mizpah, it is still appropriate for Christians to ask God's blessings on fellow believers. Maybe, instead of the Mizpah, we could use one of the benedictions that conclude the New Testament letters:

"May the Lord himself, who is our source of peace, give you peace at all times and in every way. The Lord be with you all" (2 Thess. 3:16, GNB).

"May the God who gives us peace make you holy in every way and keep your whole being—spirit, soul, and body—free from every fault at the coming of our Lord Jesus Christ" (1 Thess. 5:23, GNB).

"May God's grace be with you" (Col. 4:18, GNB).

"May God the Father and the Lord Jesus Christ give to all Christian brothers peace and love with faith" (Eph. 6:23 GNB).

"May God's grace be with all those who love our Lord Jesus Christ with undying love" (Eph. 6:24, GNB).

"The grace of the Lord Jesus Christ, the love of God, and the fellowship of the Holy Spirit be with you all" (2 Cor. 13:13, GNB).

One parting word: No benediction is worth the effort to say if it is not said in sincerity and truth. Rote and tradition are not enough.

Emmanuel L. McCall, Director
Black Church Relations Department

13
We Are Laborers Together With God
1 Corinthians 3:9

Gerald B. Palmer

The mountains had a special place in the life of Jesus. In the mountains He faced a temptation. He was offered the kingdoms of this world without the cross. On a mountain He enunciated the principles of the kingdom known as the "Sermon on the Mount." On a mountain He manifested His glory past and future on that place we call the Mount of Transfiguration. On a mountain called Calvary His blood flowed down in a crimson stream to wash our sins away. And on a mountain in Galilee He spoke for the last time on earth, giving His last command that has become the marching order of the church and is our marching order, "Go into all the world, preach, make disciples, teach them to observe all things" (see Matt. 28:19-20; Mark 16:15).

The basis of my message proceeds from the pen of the apostle Paul in 1 Corinthians 3:9, "We are labourers together with God."

The highest meaning of this passage of Scripture is the fact that we are partners *with God.* When church relationships seem to be strained, we are laborers together with God. A deacon from New Mexico once said to me, as we talked about conflict within his church and a problem with the pastor, "No preacher is too bad to keep me from going to my church."

When denominational fabric seems to pull apart we remember "we are labourers together with God." When the stress of our personal responsibilities become too great, "we are labourers together with God."

But then we are also *laborers together* with others. Paul was writing about a diverse and sometimes divided leadership, about division of responsibility and diversity of styles. We who pride ourselves on being New Testament churches must share the strengths and realities of the nature of the church. Though we recognize we are poor reeds blowing in the wind by ourselves, "together with God" we are His chosen instruments to fulfill His divine commission.

The Scripture says, "Where two or three are gathered together in my name there am I in the midst of them" (Matt. 18:20). If ever there is a miracle that occurs upon this earth, it is when individual Christians, with their diversity, their differences of opinion and background, come together in the church. His promise is: "There am I in the midst of them." Something happens! Something can happen in the Southern Baptist Convention if Christ is in our midst. Our togetherness makes it possible for us to be open to the work of the Spirit of God. Our unity doubles and multiplies our resources.

This Togetherness Is Expressed in the Churches

The church is God's primary agency for missions. This is a basic concept of the HMB. If missions is to be done across this world and across this land of ours, missions must find expression in your church and mine. Then it flows out across this nation and around this world.

People have asked, "What is the greatest result of Bold Mission Thrust?" It is that churches have caught a vision that they can be involved in that Thrust. Individuals have caught a vision that they can have their own personal bold mission venture.

We were making a hurried trip across the northern part of the United States and stopped for gas somewhere in South Dakota. A van drove up. As the door swung open I saw the name "Baptist" on the door. I asked one of the young couples where they were going. Without hesitation they reported, "We are going to Montana to build a church." There was excitement in their voices and enthusiasm in their eyes.

I was in Pennsylvania in a revival meeting recently. During the week the pastor was busy with other visitation, and I had the opportunity of spending the afternoon accompanying a member of the church in visitation. She was a tall, personable lady in her late 40s—a product of Texas Baptist work whose husband had become an executive in a company in that city—one of those families that means so much in pioneer areas. She took the lead in our visitation.

Among those we contacted was a man in his middle 40s and a graduate of Columbia University. Having served as an executive but out of work, he shared his disappointment and his discouragement. As we began to probe he said to us, "I want you to know I don't believe, but I wish I did sometimes." This woman, in a demonstration of what it means to witness, closed her discussion by saying, "Even though you do not believe I want you to know God loves you and so do we." She walked with ease, talking to the ragamuffins on the street. We visited in homes where poverty was evident. She shared the concern of a teenager's problems. Here in this city, missions seemed to have come together in the life of this woman who had made a commitment as a witness to faith in Jesus Christ. She carried out Bold Mission Thrust as well as anybody I know, and yet she would be the last to know it, let alone admit it.

We Express Our Togetherness Through
Missionary Personnel

They are our sons and our daughters. They are our church members. They are our friends. Thirty-eight-hundred-plus missions personnel serving in the homeland in fifty states, in Puerto Rico and the Virgin Islands, American Samoa, and Canada. Fifteen hundred chaplains are endorsed by the Home Mission Board. Approximately 700 Mission Service Corps persons serve together on home mission fields. Over 1,500 summer missionaries give ten weeks of their life to ministry. Missionaries serve on the exploding edges of our metropolitan areas where, in six months or a year to three years, a church may be ready to be self-supporting.

But the Yelvingtons have served in the Espanola Valley the better part of their lives, just thirty miles north of Santa Fe. Building on the work of Pauline Cammack and Mike and Rose Naranjo, they have carved out a continuing witness in the northern pueblos of New Mexico. We have been chosen to be "labourers together" with this dear couple who have served so well and so long in this difficult place.

We Express Our Partnership with God in
Southern Baptist Frontier Areas

During a revival meeting, word came to the pastor that there had been a murder in the community. Only one person out of the eight children had come in contact with the church. The man was twenty-eight years old. He had been in a tavern brawl and left on the street for dead, then run over by a hit-and-run driver. We were called to the home. It was one in a low-cost housing area. They didn't know how to talk the language of death. The mother asked, "What happens when they shut the casket? Does he know it is being closed? I'm scared. I'm scared for my boy, and I am scared to die." We asked one of the young men if he was a churchgoer. Holding a beer can in his hand, he stated the truth. "We are not church people; I guess you could call us the partying kind." The father asked, "Can't you say something to comfort us?" I watched this missionary pastor gently and firmly bear a witness to the truth and yet lay a foundation for a later witness when the truth could be proclaimed before it was too late.

This work was started by Home Mission Board missionaries and pastored by persons receiving pastoral aid from the Board. Now they were meeting in a new building overlooking the city. More than a thousand volunteers have come to this city to help build a church in this area.

Thank God for the commitment of Southern Baptists to cross into new frontiers!

In the early part of the summer I attended a special occasion in the United Nations ministry in New York City. Dr. Elias Golonka served as director of the ministry for many years before his death. Ted Mall, missionary, and Joanne Jones, US-2 worker, led in planning the occasion. Members of the United Nations secretariat and the staff of the United Nations were invited. The ministry costs are shared by the Board and state conventions. Volunteers from the association open their homes to United Nations personnel. A choir from First Baptist Church, Pasadena, Texas, presented special music. Expenses of the banquet were paid by a prominent businesswoman.

I heard the nations represented called out—Russia, Poland, Czechoslovakia, Romania, Hungary, North Yemen, Peru, Chile, Jamaica, Nigeria—almost forty countries. Southern Baptists had an opportunity to bear a general, but firm, witness to the peace that Jesus Christ brings and can bring to the world and to the love that crosses all barriers. I am proud to be a member of that partnership which makes it possible to carry on that kind of an endeavor.

Our challenge is to be missionary, to do missions. Missions is what the church does beyond itself. A church does missions as individuals reach out beyond the family of the church to those who are so close in geography, but so far away sociologically and culturally.

There is no substitute for a cool hand on a fevered brow, for the hug of a parent to a weeping child, for the steady hand on a shoulder of a discouraged person, for a listening ear to the emotionally distraught person, for the clasped hand to the terminally ill. Whether it's near or far, you are the arms of the Savior reaching out to those in need, to touch their hearts and lives and proclaim the truth of the gospel. You express the concern Jesus Christ would show if He were standing by that person. *You* are the hands of the Savior reaching out to those in need.

At Ridgecrest a couple of years ago, a blind and deaf girl was sitting in the congregation. "How can the message be communicated to her?" The girl had one hand in the hands of the interpreter. The interpreter spelled out the message being preached. The blind-deaf girl had her other hand on the face of the interpreter. She could feel the change of emotions. When the preacher told something funny, the blind-deaf girl would laugh—just a little bit after the rest. The words of the preacher became flesh in the person of this interpreter.

When Jesus Christ came into the world, "The Word was made flesh, and dwelt among us, (and we beheld his glory, the glory of the only begotten of the Father)" (John 1:14). Today we have the privilege of making the message of God's love become real to people as we share His gospel in word and deed. When we do, the meaning of the words, "We are labourers together with God," take on new significance.

Gerald B. Palmer, Vice-president
Missions
Home Mission Board

14

The Primacy of Church Starting

John 20:21

F. J. Redford

As my Father hath sent me, even so send I you.

Church starting is the primary thrust of Christian missions because Christ chose the church as His primary vehicle for evangelizing the world. The HMB operates on this basic premise. There are many fine Christian institutions (i.e., hospitals, homes for the aged, rescue missions, educational institutions), but Christ chose to establish an institution called "the church" and told that church: "As my Father hath sent me, even so send I you," to evangelize, and to minister. Christian institutions are usually the outgrowth of churches. Institutions seldom, if ever, give birth to churches, aggressively evangelize, or effectively minister in the same way and with the same degree of effectiveness as local churches.

1. *Deeds of the past indicate that church starting is the primary facet of the mission of the people called "Christians."* There are some deeds of the past, some events in history, that make this business of starting churches your business and my business as Christians. For example:

a. The deed of Christ on the cross is an event in history that overshadows all other events, secular or otherwise, in recorded history. The cross has cast its shadow across the pages of world history in such a way that even people who are not Christians are affected by that cross.

There are entire units of government, at every level, that exist because Christ came, lived, and died, saying "people are important." But I am not here to talk about politics but simply to emphasize that the crucifixion was an earth-shaking event. It is still shaking the world! It has remade the maps of the world. We sing about the cross "When I Survey the Wondrous Cross," "At the Cross," "Down at the Cross," and on goes the list of the hymns and gospel songs we love to sing about the cross. If we believe what we sing together, we must be people who are willing to start churches which share the message we sing, that Christ came, lived, loved, died, and still lives and loves that people might be reconciled to God. When we try to summarize the gospel, we say, "It is the death, burial, and resurrection of the Lord Jesus Christ." We sing about the crucifixion in the songs of the cross, we preach about it, particularly every springtime. When we constitute new churches, we adopt articles of faith that indicate a belief in the blood atonement of Christ on Calvary. Those who have taught Sunday School have presented again and again the message of the crucifixion.

If we believe what we preach, if we believe what we teach, if we believe what we sing, if we believe what we resolved in our articles of faith, if we have grown in the faith so that we understand the responsibility of the Christian, we cannot dodge the constraint that is placed squarely on our shoulders by the deed of Christ on Calvary. It is our business to plant churches to share the message of the Christ who came that we might know Him and be redeemed from sin and given life eternal.

b. *The deeds of Christians through the past several hundred years indicate that we have only met with the favor of God as we have sent missionaries and established churches.* The people called Baptists were nameless nobodies until we awakened to the missionary message of the Bible, and in 1792 sent Carey to India as our first missionary. Beginning from that time, our growth as a Christian denomination has mushroomed around the world. However, God has closed those local churches who have refused to be missionary, and has blessed with tremendous growth those who have been missionary.

In 1832 a controversy was set in motion by William Carey's previous audacity in England (in 1791) when he dared question the plight of the heathen in India. In 1832 Indiana Baptists split, and 3,000 affirmed, "The Bible is a missionary book—we must send missionaries to every geographical section of this country and the world." Three thousand protested, "No, the Lord will do it without our help; we will sit here and enjoy one another's fellowship with a monthly dinner on the ground." Fifty-two years later the Missionary Baptists of Indiana numbered 57,000; the antimissionary group had shrunk to less than seven hundred. Today you can go from Hammond, in Northern Indiana, to Indianapolis, in the central part of the state, and never see one of the antimissionary churches. To find one you have to go off the highway and back into the woods.

The same statistics tend to be found state by state, which again underscores my contention that the Lord has only blessed us as a people when we have accepted the missionary responsibility of missions, focusing on evangelism and church starting, and He has withheld His blessings and He has closed our churches when we have tried to be introverted, self-centered communities that refuse to reach out to the unchurched. So, a host of events from the pages of church history demonstrate again and again that God blesses churches when they are missionary. And, then, there are the deeds of the apostles as we read about their lives and what they did.

The journeys of the apostle Paul are familiar to all of us as we have studied them in Sunday School and in Bible classes—the shipwreck that Paul endured, the imprisonment, the abuse, the ridicule, the stoning, and the martyrdom. Yet the apostles persisted in exploring every remote corner in their day and planted new churches that people might know that Jesus Christ is both Savior and Lord. And they were doing this in response to the commission of Christ that "as my Father hath sent me, even so send I you." They were so aggressive that within the first 100 years of Christianity they moved from 120 to multiplied thousands of Christians and hundreds of churches.

So the deeds of the past again and again have underscored that starting churches, reaching out to people, is the business of every Christian in every church that started with the deed of Christ on Calvary to the deeds of all those who have served before us. It reminds me of the poem that came out of World War I. Following is an excerpt:

In Flanders fields the poppies blow
Between the crosses, row on row,
That mark our place; . . .
....
To you from falling hands we throw
The torch; be yours to hold it high!
If ye break faith with us who die
We shall not sleep, though poppies grow
In Flanders fields.

—John McCrae

I recognize that the preceding poem refers to those who died in defense of political freedom but I believe that looking on from windows of heaven are the apostles, the martyrs, and all those who served before us, those who have endured imprisonment, disease, famine, just plain hard work, and overwork through the centuries, to see how well we grasp the torch of the gospel of Christ and carry it on to greater heights for Him.

We've just established a "beachhead" for Christianity in the world. We simply have a "beachhead" in this nation. Nominally, about half the people belong to somebody's church or synagogue, out of over two hundred thirty-three million. At least a hundred million can clearly be identified as not knowing Jesus Christ as their personal Lord and Savior. We do not know how far removed many of the other so-called "churched" people are from a real relationship with Jesus Christ. Therefore, it is urgent, because of the deeds of the past, that we reach out and establish churches in every nook and cranny of our nation and of our world.

2. *We really do not have to look into the past—we can close our history books and simply open our eyes and look at the needs of the present and see that we must aggressively be about the business of starting new churches as points of evengelism and ministry in our nation and in our world.*

a. Physical needs are confronting us daily—we constantly read articles about the hungry, the homeless, and the hopelessly physically ill. As we walk or drive down streets, we see many of these miserable people. It is imperative that the church not dodge its responsibility for people who are in physical need. If everybody is to be ministered to in the name of Christ, there must be churches in every community and neighborhood where people have need for physical ministry, or they may well be inefficiently bypassed, due to the absence of a congregation that reaches out.

b. Moral needs confront us daily from the pages of our newspaper. As we open today's paper, we don't have to go beyond the front page to see the terrible moral breakdown confronting us in our nation. We see moral collapse on every hand. The news on television and radio is constantly filled with horrid stories about moral problems of various sorts and types.

c. Spiritual needs, though, seem to be basic to many of the moral and physical problems. These are all tangled together. We can't properly take care of one without the other. We have vast cities, metropolitan areas, and megapolitan areas, where we, as a major evangelical force in the nation, have not begun to do our share of the work. It is not a matter of invasion—it is a matter of being willing to share our responsibilities, as the nation's largest evangelical denomination, with resources that no other denomination in America has.

Many of the cities of America are at least two-thirds unchurched. We have exploding on the landscape in every metropolitan area—North, South, East, and West —enormous apartment and condominium complexes that the churches seem to pass by. Our congregations seem to be baffled by how to penetrate multifamily housing units. In the 1,000 counties surrounding most of our metropolitan areas, we see exploding new suburbs that are thirty or forty miles from the heart of the city, where many new subdivisions have developed and churches have not appeared to minister in those neighborhoods. Somehow we must plant churches in all these 1,000 counties that are immediately adjacent to our huge metropolitan areas.

However, at the same time, we must not abandon the

heart of these big cities where there are still multiplied
millions of people and where many churches have died
from their inability to minister to the new residents that
have come that way. We must be persistent in seeking
a way to penetrate the hardcore areas of the cities, the
baffling apartment/condominium complexes, and the
suburban areas that have been neglected. As we reflect
on the fact that at least a hundred million people in this
nation are without Christ, it is difficult to grasp the people by the millions. People are best seen one person at
a time.

Not too long ago, I was preaching in a mission church
on Sunday night, and someone knocked on the window
during the Church Training hour. We went outside to
see what was wrong, and there was a young fellow about
thirty years of age with a wife and five children in an old,
broken-down car. He was staggering around with an
empty fifth of liquor in his hand, saying, "Tell me something to keep me from going to the liquor store to get
another one of these." Two and one-half million people
are without Christ in that state. This man was one of
those two and one-half million, and he was one of the
one hundred million in the nation. He was drunk enough
to have enough nerve to knock on the church window
and say "help!" Not many people are going to do that,
are they? We are going to have to knock on their doors.
There are a lot of people staggering around in misery
because of sin and other problems. The *needs of the present*
make church starting our business. To be sure we don't
pass anybody by, we must systematically make sure that
every neighborhood is within the reach of the witness
and ministry of a New Testament church.

*The creeds of our Life demand that we be busy about the business of
planting new churches.* We, as Baptists, proudly say, "We have

no creed; we just believe the Bible." That is a lot more incriminating than the short, simple Apostles Creed, used by many of our friends of other denominations. The Bible says such things as: "The book shall be opened, and the Lamb's Book of Life shall be opened, and whoever's name is not found written in the Lamb's book of life, shall be cast in the lake of fire." (Rev. 20:15; 21:27; 22:19, Author). And we say that we believe that.

The Bible says such things as: "[Today] is the day of salvation" (2 Cor. 6:2).

The Bible says such things as: "Boast not thyself of tomorrow because you don't know whether it's going to be here or not" (Prov. 27:1, Author).

The Bible says such things as: "[Life is] a vapor that appears for a little while and then vanishes away" (Jas. 4:14, NASB).

The Bible says such things as: "The wages of sin is death; but the gift of God is eternal life through Jesus Christ our Lord" (Rom. 6:23).

And the Bible says, in the words of Christ Himself, "I am the way, the truth, and the life: no man cometh unto the Father, but by me" (John 14:6). And "[He that] climbeth up some other way, the same is a thief and a robber" (John 10:1).

We claim to believe all those verses, don't we? Most of those we quote frequently to our lost friends, trying to motivate them to accept Christ. But those same, awesome verses should come back to haunt us like an Australian boomerang. Because, if today is truly the day of salvation, if hell is so certain for the unbeliever, if life is as brief as the vapor from a teakettle, if the wages of sin is truly death, then we as Christians must be highly motivated to be extremely busy about the business of establishing points of witness and ministry within the reach of every lost, unchurched soul in every nook and corner of this nation; so there will not be one, wandering, miserable, perplexed, confused, unhappy soul that does not have the opportunity to know that Christ is truly the way, the truth, and the life.

Most of us studied *Macbeth* in school. You remember that Lady Macbeth stabbed a man, and she got blood all over her hands. She would wake people up at night stumbling around trying to scrub the blood off her hands because it was on her conscience—on her soul—this murder she had done. If we could take Lady Macbeth with her right hand to a Buddhist temple at Lahaina, Hawaii, and let her pray before that big, fat image of Buddha, she can burn all the incense she can afford before Buddha, and cook all the rice she can afford and set it on the altar by Buddha, and lay all the money she can afford on the altar in front of Buddha and pray all day, touching her head to the floor, she is still going to be getting up at night and scrubbing her hands because that big, fat image of Buddha is just going to sit there.

The monks will take the money and the rice. We could take her to a Shinto shrine and let her go through Shinto rituals and worship and burn incense, but she is still going to wake up at night screaming from nightmares, with blood on her hands. We could take her to some world-famous churches. We could take her to one and go into the pastor's study and say: "Here is a lady who has committed the sin of murder, and she can't rest night or day. She has not slept in weeks, and she has got to have freedom from this guilt." He would lean back in his swivel chair, rub his hands together, professionally, and say: "Lady, don't worry about it, there is no such thing as sin—there is no such thing as heaven or hell—just turn over a new leaf and quit killing people, and you will be all right." That's humorous to us, but it is true that such things are preached from "Christian" pulpits, and folks with sin problems don't find many answers.

We could bring Lady Macbeth to your church or anyone of 36,000 like it. From the first note of the prelude, from the first hymn of praise from a delivered heart, or from the sharing of a gospel song—she senses, *Maybe there's hope here!* Then, during prayer time, someone will pray for the seeking souls that need Christ as Savior, and she says, *They are concerned about me.* The pastor preaches. Then the invitation will be given, such as "Come, ev'ry soul by sin oppressed, There's mercy with the Lord." Lady Macbeth could walk the church aisle and give Christ her heart and become a new person in Christ Jesus, because He said, "I am the way, the truth, and the life" (John 14:6). A year from now she could be teaching a Sunday School class in your church, couldn't she? But because of what we believe Christ can do, even with a murderess, makes starting churches our business, so they will know that Christ is the way, the truth, and the life.

So, church starting is truly our business *because of the deeds of the past,* beginning with the deed of Christ on the cross, those of the apostles, the martyrs, those who have served through the centuries, the hand of God on us as a denomination when we did this—all of this indicates that church starting must be our business. And then the deeds of the present, the physical needs, the moral needs, the spiritual needs—the vast statistics of the unchurched we can't even comprehend, state by state and city by city—but, as you see, a few miserable people are symbolic of all of them, that *because of the needs of the present,* we must be busy starting churches for witness and ministry. And then the *creeds* of our life—what we say we believe about judgment, about sin, about salvation, and about Christ—makes it our business. What do we do then? Well, certainly the old answer is still very true. We can pray and we simply must have a vast undergirding of prayer support across the nation for our program of home missions, for our vast movement of starting the thousands of churches that we need to evangelize America. And we can give through the Cooperative Program and the Annie Armstrong Offering. Every time a check comes in, the Home Mission Board can enter some of these needed areas with the funds that are given. And then, many of us can go if we listen when God calls—go as He calls and work in the starting of new churches. Some challenging opportunities are right near where many Christians in America live if they could simply open their eyes and see the field that is already "white" (ripe) near them.

F. J. Redford, Director
Church Extension Division
Home Mission Board

15
Volunteerism
Personally Involved in Bold Mission Thrust
2 Kings 4:18-37

Michael D. Robertson

We have heard a great deal about Bold Mission Thrust over the past few years. The goals of reaching America for Christ and providing a New Testament church available to everyone are ambitious and highly desirable. The three-pronged approach by the Home Mission Board of evangelizing, congregationalizing, and ministry needs our prayers, financial support, and perhaps our personal involvement. Let's look at how we might become more involved in Bold Missions.

I Must Be Involved
Read 2 Kings 4:18-37

In this passage we see that Elisha had promised a child to a childless woman who had done many acts of kindness and hospitality for Elisha. The child became ill and died, so she sent for Elisha. Elisha sent Gehazi his servant, charging him to "gird up your loins and take my staff in your hand, and go your way; if you meet any man, do not salute him, and if anyone salutes you, do not answer him, and lay my staff on the lad's face" (v. 29, NASB).

He was sending Gehazi with his full authority and power as represented by the staff. He was to concentrate on the task, not to be distracted or slowed down, and to act on Elisha's behalf. But what happened? There was *no* sound or response. Sometimes we send preachers or missionaries to do the Lord's work, giving them full authority and support, but the expected results do not take place. In this passage we see that Elisha himself finally arrived, went into the house, and prayed. Then in verse 34 we read, "And he went up and lay on the child and put his mouth on his mouth, and his eyes on his eyes and his hands on his hands and he stretched himself on him; and the flesh of the child became warm" (NASB). After repeating this act we see that the child had fully recovered. It was a miracle!

But it took Elisha being personally involved, not sending someone else to do his work. It also took bold and unusual action for Elisha. For Elisha to place himself upon a corpse took a tremendous amount of faith, courage, humility, and trust. It was totally out of character for a devout Jew even to come close to a dead body, much less touch it in the way Elisha did. It violated many customs and ceremonial rites, thus making Elisha "unclean." But after prayer and persistent action he was able to bring about God's purpose.

It may take the same type of boldness and unusual action for Southern Baptists to bring about God's purpose in America! We may need to "get our hands dirty," to break with tradition, to get personally involved to reach America for Christ. Some people are already taking such action. Many are serving in one of the volunteer programs of the Home Mission Board. One such volunteer, a student summer missionary, states, "This summer I saw forty-eight young people come to know the Lord and eighty others make some other type of decision. In one way or another God directly used me in thirty of the forty-eight decisions. It's such a neat feeling to see people trust in Jesus."

Of course all of us can do something right here at home, but we must have volunteers to go where the work is not

strong enough to have local resources. We must call upon
the *"cooperative program" resource of people,* as well as finances!

I Have Been Gifted to Be Involved

The Bible does not say a lot about volunteerism as such
except for some passages in the Old Testament like Judges
5:2,9, 2 Chronicles 17:16, and Nehemiah 11:2. However,
some New Testament passages give a direct basis for what
volunteers can do and why they should be involved. Ephe-
sians 4:11-12 states, "And He gave some as apostles, and
some as prophets, and some as evangelists, and some as
pastors and teachers, for the equipping of the saints for the
work of service, to the building up of the body of Christ"
(NASB). This teaches that God has given the gifts necessary
to build His church, but not all gifts may be present in every
church. Only as we share and give are the gifts made available to everyone.

So do we all have gifts? Do I personally have something
the church needs? Romans 12:6 goes, "And since we have
gifts that differ according to the grace given to us, let each
exercise them accordingly" (NASB). Yes, each has a gift,
and, though it may be different or seemingly not as important as someone else's, we are still to use them. The gift is
not given for our personal gain or recognition, but for use
in the Lord's service.

Another summer missionary, Pam Lasley from El Dorado,
Kansas, learned to use her gift while serving in Oklahoma
City. She writes, "God showed me how to love. Before this
summer it was hard for me to show my emotions and tell
someone that I loved them. God helped me to show love to
others through my actions. He showed me how to look for
the good in people instead of the bad. Now I find myself

wanting to tell others that I love them." Yes, we have gifts and God wants us to use them.

My Involvement Can Be Meaningfully Used by God

God will take these gifts and use them to bless others. The story of the lad with a few loaves and fish as recorded in John 6:9-14 shows that even what we think to be a small or minor resource can be used greatly by God. We may be overwhelmed at the magnitude of the task and the tremendous lostness in our country and may say as the disciples did in verse 9, "What are these for so many people?" (NASB). Yet when we transform our abilities into our *availabilities*, we see that the Lord will accept our gift, bless it, multiply it, and use it to meet needs far beyond our limited vision.

Giving our gift to God also results in a blessing for ourselves. One high school volunteer said, "I feel that God is using me for the first time in my life." Another story is of roommates who were reunited on the mission field. In Michigan a lady and her husband were being given orientation by their supervisor before starting their volunteer service. He explained to them that another person, a lady from another Southern state, would be joining them the next day. When the lady arrived, the two women almost burst into tears upon seeing each other. They had been roommates in college over twenty-five years earlier, but had lost contact. What a mysterious way the Lord works!

God will also use our giving of ourselves to bless our home church. One pastor said, "This mission trip has done more to revive our church than the last three revivals we had put together!" The church is able to feel that it is a direct part of missions as it sends and supports some of its members as volunteers, even if only for a week or so. The church learns directly about missions and missionaries where perhaps earlier it had only read about missions.

God will call out from the church whom He needs to do the work. Psalm 110:3 states, "Thy people will volunteer freely in the day of Thy power, In holy array, from the womb of the dawn, Thy youth are to Thee as the dew" (NASB). Yes, young people in great numbers are to be a part, and have already been a part, of direct volunteer service. It will be God's call and in His power.

Finally, the church can help people realize God's will for their lives by supporting and encouraging volunteerism. One adult volunteer said, "I felt God calling me into missions when I was a teenager. But I got married, raised a family, and forgot about missions. Now, after all these years, I feel my volunteer service has answered God's call. Perhaps He was calling me to this all along."

Perhaps there are some today to whom God is speaking.

Note to pastor—For more volunteer stories and up-to-date statistics on volunteerism, refer to *Missions USA*, Home Mission Board annual report, Volunteer in Missions Day materials, and other references.

Michael D. Robertson, Associate Director
Special Mission Ministries Department
Home Mission Board

16
Resort & Leisure: All Things to All People
1 Corinthians 9:19-22

Michael D. Robertson

Read verse 22—"I have become all things to all men, that I might . . . save some" (RSV).

If we are to reach all people for Christ we must be willing to try different approaches, methods, techniques, etc., in order to get through to some of them. Paul did not use the same approach in every encounter. Using this as a model or example let us look at some new ideas and methods that might be utilized in reaching America for Christ.

Who Are These People?

They are people who need the gospel. Recent statistics reveal that between 50 percent and 60 percent of the people in the United States are unchurched, yet the spiritual climate is responsive. Even though these people are highly secular and have an urban mind-set, there seems to be a yearning for religion, albeit personal rather than formal. The dramatic use of new cults over the last several years demonstrates this fact. Despite the lostness of people, another survey showed that approximately 50 percent of those not now in church would attend if only someone would ask them!

The responsiveness of people is illustrated by the experience of Don Gerlach, Mission Service Corps volunteer for the HMB. Gerlach speaks of a boy he met more than a year ago. "He was from the Gilbert Islands, Tarawa, in the North-central Pacific. I talked to him, shared the gospel, and he accepted Christ. The following Wednesday I baptized him," Don recalled. "We never heard from him after that until a month ago. A young man approached me on a ship with a big smile on his face. I didn't recognize him he had changed so much. Sam told us that when he went home after becoming a Christian, all the people around his town couldn't believe the change in him. As a child he had been in trouble with the law, always drinking and fighting," Gerlach said. "In this work you can't be in a hurry," Gerlach explained. "When you go up the gangway you leave America and you must be ready to talk to everybody, from the captain to the wiper." He added, "Some people can't go aboard a ship; they can't handle it. But they can pray. They can send Bibles for those who want them so badly."

They are people whose life-styles and leisure activities take them away or keep them away from church. Many people have to work during normal church times. Many have hobbies or personal interests that keep them away over the weekend, especially sportsmen and campers.

They are rich and poor alike, but primarily those "well-off." Tourism has become a major industry in the United States with some areas or states having tourism as their top or near the top revenue producer. A few years ago a report on tourism showed that over 13.7 billion dollars were spent in the tourism industry in Texas alone.

They are people not normally reached by Southern Baptists or other churches. We traditionally reach people who are "like us," particularly in the suburbs rather than in urban areas.

Where Are They?

They are at ski slopes, beaches, campgrounds, amusement parks, theme attractions, and the like.

They are at fairs, flea markets, festivals, sporting events, arts and craft shows, etc. The rising popularity of flea markets, as many of you well can testify, is a significant "marketplace" where ministry is needed. Language festivals and agricultural festivals are drawing huge crowds. Fairs are always popular. One attempt to reach out in this particular area is that of Charles and Grace Goe. "We didn't wait for people to come to us; we made our rounds each day," Goe said. And at each booth, exhibit, or event they went to, they made friends. "People kept asking us to pray for them," Goe said. Among those seeking help were a woman whose father had died recently, a man who described himself as a "professional alcoholic," and entertainers at the fair. "Everywhere we went on the fairgrounds, there was a deep hunger for spiritual fellowship," Goe said. When people talked to him about their problems he was able to tell them, "I'm not here to judge you or what you are doing. I'm here just to help you." He was able to share with many what Christ could do in their lives.

They are at truck stops, marinas, racetracks and golf courses, on campuses and on the open road with truckers and motorcyclists. Chip Collins, a Mission Service Corps volunteer serving in Grand Junction, Colorado, has attempted to reach college students. When Chip Collins, fresh out of Southwestern Baptist Theological Seminary, came to Mesa College to direct the Baptist Student Union one year ago, he started from scratch, with only six students. "We met under a tree on the lawn for two months because they were renovating the student building," Collins recalled. But now, with more than thirty members, the Mesa College BSU even has its own house in which members hold Bible studies, fellowships, prayer breakfasts, and many other weekly student activities.

Another attempt to reach a special population has been that of home missionaries Wayne and Donnie Henderson. Wayne and Donnie were avid motorcyclists who became burdened for the gangs that roamed up and down the highways. Wayne resigned his pastorate and became a Mission Service Corps volunteer. He and Donnie ride their "bikes" to motorcycle rallies and camps and hold worship services and Bible studies for this rough and rowdy group. Through personal witnessing and just being a friend they have led many of the gang into a personal relationship with Christ.

What Can *I* Do to Reach Them?

- Get to know some of these people or groups. Try to understand their life-style and what appeals to them in their particular activities.
- Discover needs they actually have. Talk to them. Don't assume things about them or prejudge who they are. See them as people, and you will discover their hurts and needs if you are sensitive.
- Design ministries to meet these needs. Attempt to communicate in language they understand, not using church terms or the "language of Zion." For example, design a Scripture portion utilizing the theme or setting of the group or activity.
- Get personally involved and enlist others to be involved in ministries like those already mentioned or ones you can think of. Pick areas you have an interest in or are already involved in. Perhaps you can minister "as you go." Realize you can't do everything, so pick an area to concentrate in and get others to help you.

All things to all people? Yes, we must find new and creative ways to minister to various groups of people. We must
use their life-styles and special interests as avenues to communicate the gospel, not allow them to be barriers. We must
witness as we go and be bold in attempts to reach out to *all*
people, not just those "like us."

Michael D. Robertson, Associate Director
Special Mission Ministries Department
Home Mission Board

17

The Turn of the Century

Where there is no vision, the people perish (Prov. 29:18).

Oscar I. Romo

The "turn of the century" is a phrase implying that AD 2000 is in the distant future. Yet, it is only a few years until the turn of the century.

What happens in the world today will impact our nation tomorrow. Life in America continually develops in changing cultural patterns. Global influences contribute to our nation's rapidly becoming culturally interdependent.

The land that receives the world's "tired, your poor, your huddled masses yearning to breathe free" has become the "American Mosaic," a mosaic that reflects a diversity of cultural and linguistic values. In a sense, our nation is a modern Tower of Babel, a pluralistic society dispersed across an entire continent. An estimated 122 million people, excluding American blacks, have identified themselves as belonging to an ethnic/language-culture group, in addition to the 12 million internationals and 14.5 million deaf and hearing-impaired people.[1] The linguistic rhythms and intonations of the 636[2] languages used to communicate daily and the cultural uniqueness of the 500 ethnic groups make possible the composition, "America the Beautiful."

America's pluralism calls for "the development of approaches compatible with the New Testament concept of the church; yet they must permit the sharing of the gospel contextually."[3] These home mission approaches—Ethnic

Church Growth and Transcultural Outreach—use language and culture for the proclamation of the gospel.

Ethnic Church Growth seeks to establish congregations that develop into churches in the language and culture of the people. Transcultural Outreach is an effort to lead Baptist churches to reach out to all people in their community. The people determine the language usage, as the church includes all people in their various programs. Often these efforts call for classes, departments, and other activities in the language of the people.

The responsiveness of ethnic/language-culture groups to the gospel is an indication that God is at work in our nation. The initiation of new units is due to four factors:

1. The Language Missions Catalytic concept—a home mission concept which permits the catalyst the flexibility to initiate new work; assist churches in planning their growth; discover and equip leaders; develop contextual materials; work in cooperation with other Baptist entities,
2. The desire of churches, both Anglo and ethnic, to share the gospel.
3. The commitment of laypersons who have responded to the challenge and have shared their experiences.
4. The Laser Church Growth Thrust concept—a home mission concentrated effort that is flexible and adaptable and which focuses on the initiation of new work, discovery of natural leaders, strengthening the existing churches, and developing a strategy design for the future.

During the past two years the number of new units has exceeded the average for the past five years, with 348 in 1982 and 462 in 1983. The following is an effort to share an overview of selected congregations across the nation.

Houston, Texas—Hispanic

The Microcosmic Urban Strategy, a home mission concept, recommended for Houston as a result of the Laser Thrust in 1979 included a Hispanic work in the area east of I-45 and York Street. The Nueva Jerusalen (New Jerusalem) Church was started under the leadership of Joe Castillo. The Anglo church in the area was weak, so the congregation started out as a church with four families.

Today it has 250 members, with 245 in Sunday School and 265 in worship. The church uses the facilities of an Anglo church that has twenty in attendance. Nueva Jerusalen pays 90 percent of the utilities, 50 percent of the insurance, and assists with upkeep of the property. Although Nueva Jerusalen has an average of 100 professions of faith a year, it has baptized fifty new members each year. The income is approximately $90,000 a year.

Birmingham, Alabama—Deaf

The McElwain Baptist Church had an unused chapel. The deaf ministry in the city was disbursed among several churches. The deaf groups met with leaders of their churches and McElwain to request the establishment of a deaf congregation. The deaf groups pulled together, initiated their congregation, and called a pastor, Stan Stepleton, in late 1982. There were thirty members.

The group received financial assistance until the end of 1983. By January 1984 they had fifty-two members. Last year they had seventeen additions, nine of which were by baptism. The group virtually supports itself, thanks to the

graciousness of the McElwain Baptist Church that permits
them to use the chapel.

Cleveland, Ohio—Korean

The Korean congregation began in early 1981, and by that
fall Sang Hong Lee was called as pastor. The church led the
state convention with seventy-five baptisms last year. Having outgrown the facilities of the Southern Baptist church
that sponsored them, the group now meets in an American
Baptist church and is looking toward having their own
facilities. The church baptized seventy-five people in July,
1984. The trend is toward a $100,000 income in the current
year.

Visalia, California—Lahu

The Lahu people originated in China. There are less than
500,000 in China, Burma, Thailand, and Laos. Recently 250
came to Visalia, California.

A man who speaks Lahu started a congregation in August,
1984, with 100 in Bible study and sixty-eight in worship.
The socio-religious background of the people and the ability
to communicate will determine how soon this group will be
an organized church. In the meantime, they will be taught
how to function as a church.

New Orleans, Louisiana—Chinese

The Chinese churches in Houston and Memphis became
concerned that a Chinese Southern Baptist church did not
exist in New Orleans. These churches scheduled a layperson
to be in New Orleans each week during 1980. A congregation was begun; it has eighty members, fifty-two of which

are tithers. Last year they baptized fifteen people. Although the church meets in an Anglo facility, plans are to secure their own property.

Hacienda Heights, California—Korean

Begun in late 1981 under the leadership of David Han, the congregation now has 200 members. The budget is $100,000, and they have secured a building valued at $500,000.

Phoenix, Arizona—Chinese

The Laser Thrust in 1982 helped the First Chinese Baptist Church to have a vision for new work. In 1983 the church started a mission in an Anglo church located in the northern part of Phoenix. The Chinese congregation pays $200 rent, and has purchased three acres of land for $130,000. Last year they had seventeen baptisms and averaged seventy-six in Sunday School and 100 in worship.

These American-born Chinese conduct their services in English with some usage of Mandarin and with a Chinese cultural flavor. The potential of the group, composed of young professional adults, is beyond our imagination.

Often it is assumed that ethnic/language-culture congregations do not grow "fast enough." The baptism ratio of three selected states provides a bird's-eye view of the growth:

State	Asian	Hispanic	American Indian
Arizona	1.19	1.9	1.18
Oklahoma	1.5	1.4	1.12
California	1.3	1.8	————

Ethnic churches were among the top ten in baptisms in at least four states last year.

Studies indicate that an average of 345 units/congregations are begun annually and have been for the past ten years. In addition, work has been initiated with a new ethnic group each year, Thus it can be assumed that 6,210 new congregations will be established by the year 2000 and work will be begun among at least fifteen additional ethnic groups and/or languages if the present rate of growth continues. A 10 percent growth could result in more than 20,000 new congregations.

Four factors will contribute to the establishment of new work and the organizing of existing units into churches:

1. The challenging and responding of those whom God is calling to share the gospel with language-culture people in our nation,
2. The availability of contextual language materials designed to contribute to the spiritual needs of various ethnic groups,
3. The equipping of leaders in contextual settings,
4. The ability of the denomination to encourage sponsoring churches to lead the units/congregations sponsored into indigenous organized churches.

"Southern Baptists are faced with the most complex challenge in the history of Christianity as efforts are made to share the gospel contextually, thereby permitting the usage of language and culture as channels for communication. The denomination is faced with these difficult alternatives: Either—

1. Accelerate the establishment of new work;
2. Equip leaders capable of serving in America's ethnic mission field;
3. Strengthen existing language-culture congregations;
4. Provide contextual language materials;
5. Encourage participatory involvement of language-culture leaders in the life of the denomination.

Or—

1. Be content with the inability to evangelize ethnic America;
2. Lose some existing congregations;
3. Conceivably contribute to the decline of a Christian nation that currently sends the largest missionary force to share the Word globally."[4]

The world is in America. The response to this missionary challenge must be beyond the ordinary if ethnic Americans are to know of the redeeming love of Jesus Christ.

Oscar I. Romo, Director
Language Missions Division
Home Mission Board

NOTES

1. *America's Ethnicity '80s* (Atlanta: Home Mission Board, 1983), p. 45.
2. David B. Barrett, *World Christian Encyclopedia* (New York: Oxford University Press, 1983), p. 711.
3. Oscar I. Romo, "A Southern Baptist Perspective of Hispanic Missions" (unpublished paper, 1981), p. 184.
4. Romo, "Tomorrow Is Now" (unpublished paper, 1984), p. 7.

18
Why Evangelize?
Jeremiah 20:9; Acts 4:13-20
William G. Tanner

Evangelism is not optional. It is mandatory for the Christian witness and for Southern Baptists as we approach the last decade and a half of the twentieth century.

Why Evangelize?
Because of the Lateness of the Hour

World scientists have recently adjusted the doomsday clock to one minute until midnight. In essence, they are saying, "Given our nuclear capabilities, we are almost out of time!" The technology which was designed to bless us has turned out to be the greatest threat to our very existence, and the whole world is afraid that man's new power to colonize the stars will turn demonic and destructive.

Thrust into the hands of this generation in the second half of the twentieth century is potentially more perilous power than ever before entrusted to mortal man. It began on an August morning forty-one years ago as the news broke over a "war-weary" world. Over a city in Japan a lone aircraft had released a new force—an atom had been split, a city had been annihilated, 60,000 people had been killed, and nuclear energy came of age. First there was unbelief, then a deep, stunning fear, and then a vague realization that something had happened that would change forever the calloused mask of our world. It was the realization that a bomb had not been dropped on just one city, but on all the earth, and that mankind had entered a new age of unprecedented power.

Since that day our world has lumbered on uneasily, attempting to play down the bomb, to allay the fears of nuclear holocaust, to create the impression that the danger is less than the disease! But the men who opened that "Pandora's Box" in the New Mexico desert more than forty years ago do not share that illusion.

Today the men of science have become the new evangelists of "hellfire and brimstone," calling for world repentance. Listen to them: "Man now has within the range of his grasp the means to exterminate completely the human race, to scatter to the four winds in a matter of hours the civilization it has taken him so many long centuries to piece together."

Actually what we fear is not the force. Atoms are ethically neutral. What we fear is not the power, but the hands that manipulate it. What we really fear is the sinful, unregenerate heart of man. God gave us the bricks to build a "new Jerusalem," and out of them we have designed a cobalt tower and called it "Babylon!"

The total pattern of these interrelated dangers can be used by agents of darkness and secular prophets of doom to both intimidate and paralyze our initiative for national and world evangelism. Or, the very urgency of the lateness of the hour can drive us as Southern Baptists to make the sacrifices necessary to mobilize our resources for the greatest evangelistic outreach ever attempted within our global village.

But time is of the essence. Time to evangelize the burgeoning multitudes of new immigrants in our nation is running out. Time to enter underevangelized and unevangelized counties is running out. Time to reenter the inner cities that we have vacated is running out. Time to evangelize our friends and neighbors in the suburbs is running out. Time is running out for us as a denomination.

The question of the angel of the ascension is still the burning question for the church and for us today, "Why stand ye [there] gazing?" (Acts 1:10). In five hours the entire world knew about the tragic death of 269 people who died aboard the Korean Air Line flight 007 in 1984. We cannot seem to get the message out to 14 million Southern Baptists that about 67 percent of the people in this country for all practical purposes are dying without a Savior.

Some of us believe we are on the verge of a great spiritual awakening. There are others who think we are facing a very difficult time into the third millennium. No matter who is proven correct by history, our task is clear. We must evangelize, whether it is popular or not. The Home Mission Board Research Department has estimated that there are 160 million unsaved people in the United States.

Why Evangelize?
Because of the Lostness of Our Land

In the last decade many of us have ducked our heads and squinted our eyes while our nation has staggered on the brink of disaster. Morals have been democratized so that whatever the majority wants automatically becomes the norm. Ethical judgments have become relative and given away to a new hedonism, and humanism has been substituted for the Christian faith. It does not, therefore, take the keen insight of a prophet or the analytical precision of a sociological statistician to know that our's is a sinful and wicked land.

We cannot pacify the guilty conscience of a whole generation by saying, "Don't worry! To err is human. To sin is universal." We know better. The coiled chain of mankind's sin holds him in a relentless grip, and at the end of that chain is death. You can call sin anything you want to—an egotistic abnormality, psychological maladjustment, emotional sickness, mental disease, demon possession, a pathological condition—but it is still sin, and "the wages of sin is [still] death."

Evidences of the moral disintegration of our society appear in every direction. In the face of nationalized pornography, the conscience of America seems to be cauterized and paralyzed. Our Western society has become so obsessed with sin in the guise of sex that it seeps from all the pores of our national life, inciting every form of perversion and immorality. We have laws in our cities prohibiting open sewers. Why shouldn't we have laws forbiding the open cesspools of obscenities? The sewers continue to flow, majoring on destroying the moral fabric of our society until they have become the greatest threat to our society.

As Billy Graham reminds us, when a nation turns from the living God of its Christian heritage it substitutes false gods. Modern Western culture is rapidly becoming a mixture of paganism and Christianity. We have developed a sort of dual personality, a kind of quasi-religious schizophrenia. We say "in God we trust," then engrave a "me-first" philosophy on our hearts. We are no longer concerned with doing what is right but doing what is expedient. In the process we are losing our moral equilibrium.

But, thank God, there is a ray of hope in the whole miserable mess. Deep in the hearts of people there is emerging an unspoken hunger for someone or something to come to our rescue. This call is coming from a deep sense of need that has the potential of creating an unprecedented opportunity for evangelism. The very disillusionment of this hour could constitute the raw materials out of which would emerge spiritual awakening. There is one contingency. We must act decisively now.

There must be a sense of urgency concerning the "lostness of our land." Sitting until morning may be too late. Jesus knew that some things could not wait. Characterizing everything He did was a consciousness of immediacy. Regardless of what one thinks about eschatology (last things), the fact remains that man's going is imminent whether Christ comes tomorrow or whenever. That meeting in judgment is the most certain rendezvous of time, and an urgency about soul preparation for our nation should be the consuming interest of every believer. Witnessing involvement is not an option we choose—it is an imperative. It is an unavoidable obligation built into the sinful condition of our world and the redemptive nature of the Christian witness.

It may be that our evangelism needs to go back to its early antecedents—to stand for a moment with feet firmly planted on the slippery sod where the first-century Christians stood, and to sit in the arena ruins where despots and demagogues witnessed the helpless slaughter as men and women died for their faith. Her twentieth-century evangelism would receive a stern rebuke for its apathy, its mumbling complaints of hard lots, and its indifference.

If effort were suffused with imagination, we could distill from the atmosphere the words of Peter and John still ringing with frantic certainty "we cannot [help] but speak the things which we have seen and heard" (Acts 4:20). These magnificent "fools for Christ's sake," whose contagious fever reached epidemic proportions, insisted on dwelling on an aura of visions, voices, and revelations. Such concentration of devotion was like an acetylene torch penetrating the steel of a crusty dead world. Losing their direction, often they redoubled their efforts earning the ugly epitaph "fanatic!"

They set themselves on fire with the Spirit, these early first-century witnesses, and a dizzy, sin-reeling world stood up and watched them burn, amazed at their dedication. They had heard a bugle call—the one that fell from the lips of a young man who died at thirty-three, whose reveille still rang in their ears, and who never sounded the taps of defeat, not even in the seven last "notes" of the cross.

What our land needs, if it is to be evangelized, is for the word of the gospel to become a flesh-and-blood witness in the lives of 14 million Southern Baptists.

Why Evangelize?
Because We Have a Legacy from Our Lord

Perhaps the greatest single weakness in contemporary Southern Baptist life is that millions of us as born-again believers are not really involved in witnessing, and, what is worse, we do not think it strange that we are not. If the enkindling fire of salvation, which Christ said He came to light, has in any sense entered my soul, I cannot rest until I light as many other fires in the lives of others as possible. *In short, a person cannot be a Christian and avoid being an evangelist.* Witnessing is not the professionalized job of the few gifted or trained, but is instead the unrelenting responsibility of every person who belongs, even in the most modest way, to the company of Jesus.

America will be evangelized when 14 million-plus Southern Baptists with a passion for Christ and for lost people and with the world on our hearts exercise a willingness to cross all major frontiers with the gospel—when we seriously decide to get up, get out, and get on with it. The salt must get out of the salt shaker. The yeast must get into the dough. The light must shine in the darkness. And, we have got to quit carrying water to the sea and start carrying it to the desert where people are dying of thirst for lack of that Water of Life.

God did not give us a caretaker's job when He put the gospel into our hands. The world with its triumphs and its despairs, its beauty and its ugliness, its lostness and its searching, has moved next door to every one of us. We were saved to glorify the name of our Savior. We were saved that we might share with others what He has done for us personally.

And we grieve Him by our failure to witness to all people everywhere of the grace of God in Christ and in our own experience. When we are contentedly selfish and self-centered; when we are comfortably complacent and unconcerned; when we are conveniently thoughtless and indifferent; when compassion and love have forsaken us; when we can pass by on the other side of the road, leaving the lost in the ditch to die; when human needs no longer stab our consciences; when days of national peril leave us with no great sense of urgency; when we can be satisfied with "holding our own" or maintaining the status quo; when the fires of evangelism die out in our own hearts and flicker out in our churches; when judgment on a national and international scale stands at the door and we fail to recognize it; when the foundations are literally being destroyed; when Satan and the powers of darkness are having "a field day" in our land; when we are more interested in our own standing than in the glory of God; when we are more interested in statistics than in the salvation of lost people; when we are still bound by pathetic, pitiful, personal prejudice; when the reality of an eternal hell no longer flames within our hearts to give us the constant sense of deep urgency which alone can drive us on "as the people of God"—then unapologetically I say, we need to go back to the weeping prophet and listen again as Jeremiah says, "His word is in my heart like a burning fire shut up in my bones. I am weary of holding it in, indeed I cannot" (20:9, NIV).

My brothers and sisters, when we have passed by, I don't think it's going to be particularly important or significant what recognition or honors came our way, but only whether the people of our land heard and knew that there had been prophets among them with fire in their bones!

William G. Tanner, President
Home Mission Board
Southern Baptist Convention

About the Contributors

Paul R. Adkins is associate director of the Missions Ministries Division of the Home Mission Board, where he has served since 1971. The Christian Social Ministries Department has as its objective: to help churches, associations, and state conventions express Christian love and provide a Christian witness through mission ministries.

A native of Dundee, KY, Adkins is married to the former Beverly June Puckett. They have four children—Cherie, Bobbie, Beckie, and Kim.

Adkins's previous experience includes pastor/school administrator in California and Kentucky and director of the Department of Aging, Buckner Baptist Benevolences, Dallas; director of Florida Baptist Retirement Centers; secretary, Department of Christian Social Ministries, HMB; and as Christian Social Ministries Consultant/Adjunct Professor, NOBTS.

His education includes Los Angeles Baptist College (B.A.), Whittier College, Claremont Men's Graduate School, Carver School of Missions & Social Work, SBTS (M.A.); University of Louisiville, SBTS, University of Michigan, and NOBTS (Ed.S., Ed.D.).

Robert T. Banks, Jr., is executive vice-president for administration of the Home Mission Board. He assists the president, Dr. William G. Tanner, in the area of agency administration, interagency relationships, internal operations, and financial affairs.

He is from Griffin, GA, and he and his wife, the former Martha Sibley, have three children.

Before coming to the HMB in 1981, he served many years in Royal Ambassador and Brotherhood work—as RA secretary in Oklahoma, as Brotherhood director in Oklahoma, as executive assistant to the executive director of the Brotherhood Commission, as director of the program section, Brotherhood Commission.

He is a graduate of Baylor (B.A.) and SWBTS (M.R.E.).

M. Wendell Belew, with the HMB since 1956, serves as director of the Missions Ministries Division, assuming this position in 1971. In his division are four departments of missions—Christian Social Ministries Centers, Interfaith Witness, Special Mission Ministries, and Black Church Relations. Nearly 40,000 volunteers and 600 missionaries serve through this division.

Belew, a native of Keefer, KY, was a Lt. Line officer in the U.S. Navy, World War II. He served as pastor and then as director of mountain missions, Kentucky Baptist Convention, before coming to the HMB. His positions with the HMB have been director, Church-centered Missions, secretary, Department of Associational Missions, secretary, Association Administration Services/Church Extension Division, secretary of Pioneer Missions, and his current assignment.

He and his wife, nee Edna Record, have three children. His education includes the University of Kentucky, Georgetown College (B.A., D.D.), and SBTS (B.D.).

He has been president of the American Society of Missiology and is on the board of managers, American Bible Society. He is the author of nine books, including Broadman's *Churches and How They Grow* and *The Dark's A-Creepin'*. He has been honored with the Victor T. Glass Award for racial reconciliation.

Robert Eldon Bingham joined the HMB staff in 1972 as vice-president, Services Section. He provides administrative supervision for the Services Section (Personnel, Communications, and Business Services) in undergirding all the work of the Board and provides staff leadership in public relations and in furthering financial support.

A native of Kansas City, MO, he is a graduate of the University of Kansas (B.S.), and has done additional work at Furman University and Union Theological Seminary. He is married to the former Opha Stump, and they have two daughters.

He served three churches as minister of education before coming to the HMB (First Baptist, St. Joseph, MO, First Baptist, Greenville, SC, and Wieuca Road, Atlanta).

He was in the U.S. Navy during World War II. He has been the Gheens Lecturer at SBTS, and has served as adjunct professor at MWBTS. He has written more than 200 articles for SBC publications and has done seven books, including Broadman's *Traps to Avoid in Administration* and *One Step More, Lord!* by Opha Bingham (with Robert E. Bingham).

David Thomas Bunch is director of Mission Service Corps, HMB. His work is to locate mission areas which would benefit from volunteer assistance and enlists and assigns long-term volunteers to work in these areas.

He was born in Eldon, MO, and is married to Norma Joann DeLozier. They have two children.

He was educated at Southwest Baptist College (now U.) with an A.A., William Jewell (B.A.), Central Baptist Seminary, Kansas City (B.D. and Th.M.), and MWBTS (D.Min.).

He served as pastor in Missouri (Sedalia, Turney, Florissant, and St. Louis) and as pastoral missionary in SD and area director of missions in Iowa before coming to the HMB.

He has held many positions in his denomination, especially on the state level.

Joe Ford was associate vice-president, Evangelism, Home Mission Board, Atlanta, GA, having joined the HMB staff in 1974. He recently accepted the call of the North Phoenix Baptist Church, Phoenix, AZ, to serve as co-pastor.

A native of Fort Worth, Texas, he is a graduate of East Texas Baptist College, Marshall, TX (B.A.), and SWBTS (M.Div., D.Min.). He is married to the former Charlotte Cunningham of Valdosta, GA, and they have two children.

His background includes youth director in Texas and Louisiana churches, youth evangelism, the pastorate in Oklahoma, associate in the evangelism department, Baptist General Convention of Oklahoma; director of evangelism for young adults,

Adult Evangelism Department, HMB; interim pastor of nine churches in Georgia, director, Evangelism Development Division, Evangelism Section, HMB; and acting v.-p., evangelism section.

He has written for many denominational periodicals. He received the W. T. Trady Service Award, East Texas Baptist College.

Alfred Carl Hart was director of the Chaplaincy Division of the Home Mission Board. He joined the staff in 1970 and served as the associate director of Institutional Chaplaincy until becoming director of the Division in 1977. Prior to coming to the HMB, he served as director of chaplaincy in the Tennessee Department of Corrections. He has pastored in North Carolina and Tennessee.

He is married to the former Janie Sue Davis. They have two sons, David Carl and Paul Alfred. He attended Union U. (D.D. from Union in 1981), Bethel College (B.A.), SEBTS (M.Div.), Emmanuel Baptist College (D.D.), and has done postgraduate courses at Mental Health Center, Memphis; Georgia Baptist Hospital, Atlanta; West Georgia College, and Oglethorpe U. He recently joined the Motor Convoy, Inc., of Atlanta as director of Chaplain Services.

He has served in the Navy and has written many materials in the area of institutional chaplaincy and corrections.

Robert Lee Hamblin, a native of Hamilton, Ohio, has served as vice-president, Home Mission Board, Evangelism, since 1982. Before then he was professor of evangelism at NOBTS. He directs and administers the Evangelism Section and relates evangelism programs to other HMB and SBC programs.

He is married to the former Mary Ruth Miller. They have three children. He has been educated at Union University (B.A.; later LL.D.), SWBTS (B.D., Th.D., Ph.D.) and received an honorary D.D. from Mississippi College. He has published two books with Broadman, *The Spirit-filled Trauma* and *Triumphant Strangers: A Contemporary Look at 1 Peter.*

He has pastored the Elliston B. C., Memphis, and the Harrisburg B. C., Tupelo, MS.

Richard H. Harris is director of the Mass Evangelism Department, HMB. He has the responsibility of managing the department through supervision of department personnel in planning, budgeting, and performing the work of the department within the guidelines, policies, and budget of the HMB. He gives leadership to the department in the developing and implementing of mass evangelism programs and strategies in five areas: revivals, crusades, prospect discovery, media evangelism, and as the HMB Liaison for SBC vocational evangelists.

He hails from Somerset, KY. He is graduate of Cumberland College, KY (B.S.), Eastern Kentucky State U. (M.A.), and SWBTS (M.Div., D.Min.). He is married to the former Nancy Metcalf. They have two children. He has served as recreational staff intern, First B. C., Dallas; as pastor in Texas, and as consultant for evangelism departments in Texas and Kentucky; as associate director, Mass Evangelism Department, Evangelism Section, HMB; and in his current position since 1983.

He has written widely in the area of evangelism.

Leonard Gayle Irwin joined the staff of the HMB in 1960. He is vice-president, Home Mission Board, Planning. He provides management for the Planning Section and leadership in planning, budgeting, and research.

He is a native of Pensacola, FL, and was educated at Auburn U. (B.S.), NOBTS (M.Div., M.R.E.), Butler U., and Georgia State U.

He and his wife, the former Johnnie McDonald, have two children. He has served as an analysis engineer for the Gulf Power Co., Pensacola, FL. He pastored three churches before coming to the HMB. He previously served as associate secretary, Survey and Special Studies Department, HMB, and then as secretary, Survey and Special Studies Department.

Emmanuel Lemuel McCall, Sr., has been director of the Black Church Relations Department since 1975. In this capacity he gives leadership to the Southern Baptist Convention's cooperative ministries with National Baptists, to the development of black Southern Baptist churches, and to ministries of racial reconciliation.

He is a native of Sharon, PA. He is a graduate of the University of Louisville (B.A.), SBTS (M.Div., M.R.E.), and Emory U. (D.Min.). He and his wife, the former Emma Marie Johnson, have two children, Emmanuel, Jr., and Evalya.

Before coming to the HMB he was associate pastor of Joshua Tabernacle B. C., Louisville; pastor of 28th Street B. C., Louisville; and professor at Simmons Bible College. Before becoming director of the BCRD, he was associate. He has authored three books, the latest being *Black Church Life-styles* (Broadman). He has two honorary D.D. degrees.

Gerald Burton Palmer joined the staff of the Home Mission Board in 1960 as associate secretary in the Language Missions Division. He is now vice-president, Missions, and he provides administrative leadership to the divisions and departments of the Missions Section and correlates the work of this section with other groups both inside and outside the Board.

He was born in Minneapolis, MN, and is a graduate of Northwestern Bible School and Seminary (Dip. and Grad.Th.) and Hardin-Simmons U. (B.A., also D.D.). He is married to the former May Elizabeth (Libby) Black, and they have four children.

He has been an associational missionary, a pastor, director of Spanish and Indian work, HMB, NM; and director of missions, Baptist Convention of NM.

He has authored a study book entitled *Winds of Change.*

Francis Jackson Redford serves as director of the Church Extension Division of the Home Mission Board, Atlanta, GA. His division coordinates and promotes the starting of new churches and missions in old and new convention areas, bringing them to self-support.

He was born in Memphis, TN, and is married to the former Mildred Evans. They have four children.

He was educated at Decatur Baptist College, TX (Dip.), Howard Payne U. (B.A.), Hardin-Simmons (residence requirement for M.A.), SWBTS (B.D.), and Linda Vista Bible College and Seminary (D.D.).

He served churches in TX and AR was a chaplain in the Army for two hitches. He has been pastor and area missionary, IN, and secretary for the Department of Missions, State Convention of Baptists in IN. He has served the HMB as associate sec., Department of Pioneer Missions and director of Church Extension Department before his present stint. He has been visiting professor of missions at five of our seminaries—SEBTS, SWBTS, MBTS, GGBTS, and SBTS.

Planting New Churches was his book for Broadman in 1979.

Michael David Robertson is associate director of the Special Mission Ministries Department. He joined the HMB staff in 1976.

He coordinates work of consultants and missionaries in areas of resort missions, special events, creative arts, experimental ministries, and adventure missions; administers department budget; chairs the US-2 committee; and coordinates department communications and data processing.

He is a native of Cape Girardeau, MO. He is a graduate of Memphis State U. (B.S.), SBTS (M.Div.), and Murray State U. (graduate work toward M.A.). He is married to the former June Crane of Memphis, TN. They have two children.

He has served as summer missionary and on the Glorieta staff, as systems analyst/computer programmer, for Continental Oil, as a US-2 missionary, as a minister of youth, as campus minister, Murray State U. He came to the Board as assistant director, Special Mission Ministries Department, HMB. He has written many articles for magazines like *The Student, Church Recreation, The Baptist Program, Royal Service, Church Training,* and others.

Oscar I. Romo serves as director of the Language Missions Division of the HMB, where he came in 1971. He directs the work of ministering to non-Anglo populations in the U.S. and starting new missions and churches with ethnic groups. The work of the division includes refugee ministry and resettlement and ministry to seamen. He continues to encourage Southern Baptist leaders and church members to recognize the U.S.'s growing ethnicity and to include ethnic persons in their growth plans and leadership responsibilities.

He is a native of Lockhard, TX. He and his wife, Zoe Harmon, have two children. He has pastored churches in Texas and was associate, language missions department, Baptist General Convention of Texas. He came to the Board as assistant secretary, Language Missions Department, HMB.

He also served as an army chaplain and has been adjunct professor at GGBTS and MBTS. He has written widely in Spanish and English. He has edited *El Boletin Bautista, El Estandarte Bautista* (Spanish edition of *The Baptist Standard*).

William G. Tanner is president (formerly executive director-treasurer) of the Home Mission Board, coming to that position on January 1, 1977. As president, Dr. Tanner provides leadership for the Board's finances and programs of work: Associational Administration Services, Metropolitan Missions, Rural-Urban Missions, Chaplaincy, Christian Social Ministries, Church Extension, Black Church Relations, Evangelism Development, Mass Evangelism, Personal Evangelism, Interfaith Witness, Language Missions and Church Loans. The HMB ministers in all fifty states, Puerto Rico, and American Samoa.

He is a native of Tulsa, OK. He is married to the former Ellen Sampey Yates. They have four children. He pastored churches in Wheelock, Cleburne, and Houston, TX, and First Baptist Church, Gulfport MS. He served as president of Mary Hardin-Baylor College and then Oklahoma Baptist U.

He is a graduate of Baylor U., B.A., later L.L.D., the University of Houston (M.Litt., Ed.D.), SWBTS (B.D., Th.D., replaced by Ph.D.), California Baptist College awarded him the D.M., the University of Richmond awarded him the D.D., and Campbell U. awarded him the L.H.D. He is a member of many professional and denominational committees including the Executive Committee, Last Frontier Council, BSA; Southern Baptist Historical Society, North American Baptist Fellowship, Baptist Joint Committee on Public Affairs, and the Executive Council of the Baptist World Alliance, chairman Education Commission of the SBC. He received SWBTS's Distinguished Alumni Award in 1976. He is the author of many articles and of Broadman's *Hurry Before Sundown*.